HISTORY OF THE LEAGUE FOR INDUSTRIAL RIGHTS

A Da Capo Press Reprint Series

CIVIL LIBERTIES IN AMERICAN HISTORY

GENERAL EDITOR: LEONARD W. LEVY

Claremont Graduate School

HISTORY OF THE LEAGUE FOR INDUSTRIAL RIGHTS

By Walter Gordon Merritt

DA CAPO PRESS • NEW YORK • 1970

A Da Capo Press Reprint Edition

HD 8055.L4 M4 1970

This Da Capo Press edition of
History of the League for Industrial Rights
is an unabridged republication of the
first edition published in New York in 1925.

Library of Congress Catalog Card Number 76-120852
SBN 306-71961-4

Published by Da Capo Press
A Division of Plenum Publishing Corporation
227 West 17th Street, New York, N.Y. 10011

HISTORY OF THE
LEAGUE FOR INDUSTRIAL RIGHTS

BY

WALTER GORDON MERRITT

LEAGUE FOR INDUSTRIAL RIGHTS
165 BROADWAY, NEW YORK CITY

1925

FOREWORD

❡ The History of the League for Industrial Rights is a part of the History of the United States. It deals with two decades of legal and political contest over industrial issues too little understood—too little considered. This contest has been so fraught with dramatic events, closely related to the daily life of our people, that a durable record of them was needed for this and future generations.

❡ Those who wish to form a fair and intelligent judgment on some of the most controversial and perplexing of our industrial questions, can ill afford to be ignorant of the contents of this little volume.

The Publishers

HISTORY OF THE
LEAGUE FOR INDUSTRIAL RIGHTS

INTRODUCTORY

Individual character, incentive, and responsibility are still believed to be the cornerstones of our social structure. Faith in men as individuals, exalted above faith in their institutions, organizations, groups, or classes, was the outstanding faith of the founders of our republic and continues today as the faith of their descendants. For this, the founders were criticized as radical; for this their descendants are criticized as conservative. This political and social faith explains why our constitution limits the power of the majority to override minorities; why our laws sanction labor litigation to protect industrial liberty; why, in these particulars, the United States differs from all other nations; why, as many people believe, constructive economic effort in the United States surpasses that of other nations.

Notwithstanding some tendencies toward regulation and organization the last two decades of political and legal contest in the United States, between organized forces, actuated by conflicting social and economic philosophies, have finally resulted in a confirmation in some conspicuous features, of industrial liberty and industrial individualism. While some other nations have drawn away from such conceptions, the United States has bound itself more closely to them. The important part which the American Anti-Boycott Association, rechristened the League for Industrial Rights in 1919, has played in all this, is a story which should now be told.

HISTORY

BEGINNING
Two men were slowly walking along a wood road which wound its way toward the top of a Connecticut hill. With them was a younger man of the next generation—a college undergraduate. As the road turned and a vista opened, they paused for breath, and continuing a conversation which had been earnest and uninterrupted, one of them suddenly remarked: "Why not form an organization of employers to fight these union abuses and protect industrial liberty?" That turn in the old wood road was the birthplace of the League for Industrial Rights. That vista was the inspiration. The two men who were conversing were Charles H. Merritt and Dietrich E. Loewe, both of Danbury; their companion, Walter Gordon Merritt, who afterwards became Associate Counsel for the League.

That fateful walk up the Connecticut hill

4

took place in 1901. From then on, this idea of a new organization grew in the minds of these two men, and, being men of resolution and themselves threatened by union abuses in the hatting industry, they undertook to make their dream a reality.

In those days, the popular conception of industrial rights was far different from what it became after twenty years of activity on the part of the organization then in contemplation. The law was undeveloped. Legal relief from union abuses was comparatively unknown. It almost never happened that the aggrieved party sought protection in the courts. It is true that in the so-called Debs case in 1894 the government sought an injunction against the American Railway Union to prohibit interference with the railroads and to prevent discrimination against the so-called "scab cars" of the Pullman Company. A few other cases had also been started by private parties, but they represented merely the exception that proves the rule. There was no great body of jurisprudence dealing with labor litigation. Industrial rights were undefined, and no one knew what would come to be the legal limitations on the power of combinations to obstruct the rights of individuals. No one knew that this country, unlike all others, was to embark on a unique course of labor litiga-

THE LAW WAS UNDEVELOPED

tion—a course which England has since expressly renounced. Employers and employes alike shared the belief that labor unions, being voluntary associations, were not suable or responsible and that relief was unobtainable in the courts.

THE BOYCOTT OF THE A. F. OF L.

At that time the American Federation of Labor was conducting boycotts against employers throughout the length and breadth of the nation. In 1882 the Organized Trades and Labor Unions of the United States and Canada, which was the predecessor of the American Federation of Labor, passed a boycotting resolution which Mr. Gompers assisted in framing. In 1886 the first Constitution of the Federation provided that: "It shall be the duty of the Executive Council to secure the unification of all labor organizations, so far as to assist each other in any justifiable boycott."[1] A committee on labels and boycotts was promptly established. In 1887, the "New York Tribune" and the W. L. Douglas Shoe Company were both placed on its boycott list. From then on it became the systematic business of the Federation to boycott a large number of concerns. In 1889, the secretaries of all affiliated unions were instructed to report to the president every three

[1]Report of Proceedings of the 1st Annual Convention of the American Federation of Labor, 1886, p. 4.

months a list of the addresses of their secretaries for the purpose of sending out boycott and other circulars. On one occasion, action was taken against an affiliated union for refusing to endorse one of the Federation boycotts. The system grew apace. In January, 1897, eighty-three firms were listed as *"unfair"*. Later 80 to 100 concerns appeared on each monthly list. The Federation saw the danger of diffusing its efforts in this way, and recommended "That, in order to attain the highest degree of success, we should concentrate our efforts upon a few of the concerns which have proven themselves unfair."[1] The Federation regarded this activity so important that in a boycott case in the United States Supreme Court it filed a petition declaring that a decision in favor of the plaintiff in that case "would seriously obstruct and hinder the American Federation of Labor in carrying out the purposes for which it was organized." Mr. Gompers declared that he believed in the principle of the boycott even though "it starved a man to death."

Vigorous action was necessary to make a boycott effective. An unfair list, published in the "Federationist", the official organ of the American Federation of Labor, was sent to all affiliated bodies and agents of the Federation

---

[1] Report of Proceedings of the 17th Annual Convention of the American Federation of Labor, 1897, p. 43.

with exhortations to do their utmost. Fifteen hundred boycotting agents, some 30,000 local unions, 29 state federations representing the unions in a particular state, and over 500 central trades councils representing the unions in their particular cities, thus had their cooperation enlisted. Labor union spies ascertained the manufacturers' shipments, and wired the trades council at the point of consignment to prevent the purchaser from receiving them. Destroying business was made a business, and the space devoted to it in official publications of the American Federation of Labor indicate that it was regarded as a major business.

INDUSTRIAL LAWLESSNESS

But this was not the only kind of obstruction and interference practised by labor unions which went unremedied in 1902. A system was also under way to strike against the use of all manufactured products not union made. Likewise when violence, intimidation, and picketing followed strikes, when non-union men were driven from their trade, or when contracts were broken at the instigation of a militant union, protection was largely dependent on the doubtful willingness of the public prosecutor—often a man influenced by political considerations. In extreme cases, troops were called in, and, if adequate protection were otherwise unobtainable, watchmen, or so-called guards, were employed by the employer at his own expense.

This was the picture of industrial lawlessness which these two Connecticut men saw when they reflected on the formation of a protective organization. Also they saw that these uncurbed activities of labor unions and the apparent defenselessness of industry directly concerned them. The hatters' union above all others was making such effective use of the boycotting machinery of the American Federation of Labor that only about ten hat manufacturers remained open shop. The rest had succumbed. Already it had become a common rumor in the industry that the remaining few would be taken one by one like the victims in the past. "Der Tag" could not be far off.

Steps to organize a defense organization were at once taken. A meeting of the remaining champions of the open shop in the hatting industry took place in February, 1902, at the office of Charles Biggs, Actuary for the hatting industry, 13 Astor Place, New York, at which it was decided to address a letter to the long list of names recorded on the unfair list of the American Federation of Labor. It was thought these victims of a common peril would be most ready to respond. The letters were written and at the next meeting the replies were classified as to those who voted for

ORGANIZING THE DEFENSE

a defense organization and those who voted against it. After the tally was made, it was announced that the "noes" had it. Discussion followed as to whether it was desirable to proceed in the face of such a discouraging response from the very men under attack. The entire program hung in the balance, when one of the two men we have seen climbing the hill spoke. "The 'noes' may have it," he said, "but we will take the 'ayes,' and, using them as a nucleus, will proceed to build a larger organization. Let us go forward." The others assented, as so often men do when a leader speaks. The organization of the American Anti-Boycott Association was thus assured.

This little band of hat manufacturers then underwrote the expense of employing Mr. Daniel Davenport, an attorney in Bridgeport, to enlist the interest of a substantial number of large concerns to attend an organization meeting. Mr. Davenport set upon his difficult task. He often remarked that, in his efforts to establish this infant organization, he trod more miles than did St. Paul to establish the infant church. He wondered whether, for the first time, he had set himself too big a task. But that tenacious purpose, obvious to every one who has looked upon Mr. Davenport's face, was not to be gainsaid.

On September 18, 1902, a preliminary meeting of twenty-seven manufacturers took place in New York City. A small group of pioneers were they, representing twelve industries, but not one of them from a so-called trust or any of the small group of the largest industrial organizations. Yet they set out to shape the industrial institutions of the country, and unanimously resolved that an association should be formed to enforce the law in connection with industrial relations. "Organized violation of law must be met by organized enforcement of law"—"A just man armed is potent for peace"—these were their slogans.

A temporary organization committee was created, and on October 2nd the group again met to hear its report. Mr. Biggs was appointed Temporary Confidential Agent, and Mr. Davenport was instructed to interview other manufacturers. Meetings followed in November and December of the same year, and on December 2nd the General Committee adopted a constitution with a preamble which read: "The undersigned, aware of the far-reaching consequences and dangerous extent of the boycott, threatening capital by arbitrary proscription and labor by tyrannical persecution, form themselves into an association."

The program of the new organization presented a difficult target for unfriendly critics. "A servant of greed, doing a nasty despicable

THE PURPOSE

11

job," says Mr. Gompers, "Casting about for a stone to fit its sling, it has selected the law."[1] In other words the head and front of the offending was to enforce the law, and it is not a bad idea to have the laws enforced. Labor unions have stimulated the enforcement of labor laws. No one disputes that. The new organization resolved that when the liberties of men in industry were assailed by unlawful acts, the protection of the courts should be invoked. Subsequently, when the courts began to function and the unions made political efforts to exempt their activities from legal restriction, the new organization also played an important part in defeating these efforts. Its founders believed that individual responsibility and individual incentive,—the cornerstones of our social structure,—should not be overridden by group responsibility and collectivism, and they were prepared to defend that belief through the preservation and enforcement of certain principles of law.

LAUNCHING THE NEW ORGANIZATION

It was a requirement of the constitution of the American Anti-Boycott Association that there be 100 charter members before the organization should be launched. By April, 1903, these were secured, and a temporary general executive committee appointed to complete the details of organization. The

---

[1] *American Federationist*, March, 1921, p. 232.

membership was classified into groups, and in May the temporary committee was succeeded by a permanent board of twenty, representing twenty different industries. Mr. Charles H. Merritt was elected Chairman of the General Executive Board, a position which he held until his death, April 4th, 1918, and Mr. Rudolph Blankenburg—who later became the "Reform Mayor" of Philadelphia—and two others were elected vice-chairmen. In June, Mr. Biggs was formally elected secretary.

Field men or solicitors were employed to **TIMIDITY** enlarge the organization. Membership grew, —slowly to be sure. A vague fear which played a strong part with business men in those days led many to refuse interviews with these solicitors except under conditions of great secrecy. Membership in the new organization had to be confidential because men were afraid that the union machinery would be turned against them if their membership were disclosed. Some members, not even satisfied with this, sent their contributions through an attorney, so that their name would not become a part of the Association records. Magazines and newspapers contributed to this fear by being hesitant and timid in their treatmen of the subject. Outspoken views, such as one hears today from business men on this subject, were exceptional in these early days.

Men now find the labor question no less ominous than twenty years ago, but they have grown accustomed to talk more openly, concerning it.

EARLY RECOGNITION

The Association soon won prestige among those accustomed closely to observe national developments as is evidenced by the early testimonial of Charles W. Eliot, president of Harvard University, who said:

"In the interests of good will between employers and employed, the strong Anti-Boycott Association, which was organized last year, is to be welcomed in spite of the fact that its membership is secret. It has already proved to be an effective combatant, and all people of good will may wisely wish it success in defeating and ultimately eliminating the boycott as conducted by the American Federation of Labor or other numerous bands of unionists."

THE FIRST CASE

Naturally enough this new organization was not long in existence before there came the first cry for help from a member. Naturally enough it came from Chicago. The Kellogg Switchboard and Supply Company of that city was in distress. It employed about 800 people, and had been handed a closed shop agreement by the unions of electrical workers, machinists, brass workers, and brass molders, which it refused to sign. On May 7th, 1903, a strike was called, followed by picketing, rioting, intimidation, and violence.

Then the teamsters' union undertook a general boycott. Sympathetic strikes were threatened. Teaming contractors were forced to refuse to haul the output of the company. Express companies were about to discontinue service. The company was beleagured. Mr. Daniel Davenport, as counsel for the American Anti-Boycott Association, arrived in Chicago, and publicly served notice that he was there to enforce the law, and that the existing combination violated the criminal laws of both the state and nation. A meeting of 500 delegates from the different unions in Chicago gathered in noisy protest against courts, police, public officials, and injunctions, but another public announcement by counsel had a salutary result. The result was dramatic. The boycott ceased.

On May 25, 1903, an application for an injunction had been made to the state court to stop further interference. Numerous affidavits were submitted showing violence and disorderly acts to prevent the conduct of the business. The injunction was granted, and was affirmed on appeal.

Violations of the injunction compelled the

complainant to start contempt proceedings. All of the accused, except one, were found guilty, most of them receiving jail sentences. The case finally came before the Supreme Court of Illinois, where the defendants urged that the injunction was void because it infringed on "the right to trial by jury and of free speech." On June 22, 1905, the court rendered its decision. It declared that "the importance and far-reaching consequences of the cases are fully appreciated," and held the injunction was proper.

The demand for the closed shop was discussed, and it was decided that such a contract signed under threat of strike would be under duress and voidable. Fundamental liberties were defined:

"The law is well settled that every person shall be protected in the right to enter into contracts or in refusing to do so as he shall deem best for the advancement of his own interests, without interference by others. No person or combination of persons can legally, by direct or indirect means, obstruct or interfere with another in the conduct of his lawful business, and any attempt to compel an individual, firm, or corporation to execute an agreement to conduct his or its business through certain agencies or by a particular class of employes is not only unlawful and actionable, but is an interference with the exercise of the highest civil right. * * * There can be no doubt that any attempt to coerce the Kellogg Switchboard and Supply Company into signing said agreement by threats to order a strike was unlawful. It was violative of the clear legal right of the Company, and was unjust and oppressive as to those who did not belong to the labor organizations."

This was the first case of its kind ever carried to the highest court of Illinois, and it laid the foundations of the law in that great industrial state which would operate as a bulwark for many years to follow. As years have gone by, its value has been realized by the many times it has been cited as a precedent in Illinois and elsewhere.

A sad event occurred in connection with this case. In July, 1904, Mr. A. C. Allen, an attorney who represented the Kellogg Switchboard and Supply Company, entered an elevator in a building on LaSalle Street just west of the City Hall. Except for the elevator boy, the only other person present was a man who apparently like himself was a passenger. While in the elevator Mr. Allen was beaten into unconsciousness and left for dead. The fellow passenger had done it and fled. The American Anti-Boycott Association, with

COUNSEL ASSAULTED

others, offered a reward for the apprehension of the guilty party. Suspicion rested on Black-jack Gallagher, a well-known labor slugger, who was indicted, arrested, and let out on bail, but a trial resulted in an acquittal because of lack of satisfactory identification. It was many months before Mr. Allen began to recover his faculties. He abandoned the practice of law in Chicago.

OTHER CHICAGO CASES

Other litigation developed in Chicago at this time in connection with these same difficulties. Twelve damage suits with claims aggregating $131,000 were instituted. The new organization promptly flew to the rescue of a small painting contractor who was being crushed by a powerful group of unions. But even an allusion to these may be misplaced, if one is to sidetrack detail, and clearly portray the larger issues which became an important item in the contemporaneous history of the country.

IN MARYLAND

One of the earliest ventures of the Association was in the courts of Maryland. In 1903, John B. Adt, a manufacturer of machinery, particularly for Baltimore brewing companies, received a demand from My Maryland Lodge No. 186, which was instigated by the Baltimore Federation of Labor. On July 1st the machinists struck. A committee from the Baltimore Federation declared it would place the concern on the unfair list, and would prevent people from working there unless it yielded. It picketed the place, appointed spies to follow the wagons and workmen in order to discover where work was being done, and threatened customers with the boycott. Some breweries were boycotted because they purchased machinery from Adt, and threats of like action caused others to discontinue patronage. The company sought relief in the courts, and on June 11th, 1904, an injunction was issued. The defendants appealed, and the highest court of Maryland, in overruling their contentions said:

"The right of an individual to carry on his business as he sees fit and to use such implements or processes of manufacture as he desires to use provided he follows a lawful avocation and conducts it in a lawful manner, is entitled to as much consideration as his other personal rights; and the law should afford protection against the efforts of powerful combinations to rob him of that right and coerce his will by intimidating his customers and destroying his patronage."

Already the stage was being set for a far greater battle. Forces were lining up for a national struggle over an issue which led to a *cause celebrè*. In the summer of 1902 a pamphlet by Walter Gordon Merritt entitled

PRELUDES TO THE HATTERS' CASE

19

"The Neglected Side of Trade Unionism" was privately published and circulated, and led to considerable comment. It presented to the public for the first time a complete picture of the boycotting machinery of the American Federation of Labor, and its story found an interested reception. So much attention did it command that Mr. Gompers was unable to ignore it. In the November issue of the "American Federationist," he published one of his vigorous and inimitable editorials entitled "The American Federation of Labor and the Boycott." He declared that thanks to the pamphlet "a truly wonderful and pickwickian discovery"[1] had been made by a certain section of the press. He referred to the system of boycotting, declaring "why, this may spell ruin and bankruptcy to the boycotted! Certainly it may."[2] With an outcry of defiance he threw down the gauntlet: "We beg to say plainly and distinctly to Mr. Merritt and his fellow-sympathizers that the American Federation of Labor will never abandon the boycott and that the threats against the Federation are idle, impudent and impotent."[3]

Even as the challenge of the Federation was uttered, a small coterie of men gathered in

---

[1] American Federationist, November, 1902, p. 808.
[2]   "   "   "   1902, p. 809.
[3]   "   "   "   1902, pp. 808-9.

New York, forged the instrument with which to meet it.

Another event of national importance added to public interest in these matters. The anthracite coal strike of 1902 threatened the public with privation and led to much disorder. After it had dragged on for many months, President Roosevelt by vigorous action prevailed upon the parties to accept arbitration, and appointed the Anthracite Coal Strike Commission for that purpose. The award rendered in March, 1903, with simplicity and decisiveness, declared emphatically for the open shop:

> "That no person shall be refused employment or in any way discriminated against on account of membership or nonmembership in any labor organization; and that there shall be no discrimination against or interference with any employe who is not a member of any labor organization by members of such organization."

The boycott received similar treatment. The Commission declared it had a "duty to condemn another less violent, but not less reprehensible, form of attack upon those rights and liberties of the citizens which the public opinion of civilized countries recognizes and protects. * * * What is popularly known as the boycott (a word of evil omen and unhappy origin) is a form of coercion by which a combination of many persons seek to work their will upon a single person or upon a few persons by compelling others to abstain from social or beneficial business intercourse with such person or persons. Carried to the extent sometimes practiced in aid of a strike and as was in some instances practiced in connection with the late anthracite strike, it is a cruel weapon of aggression and its use immoral and anti-social."

These utterances did much to crystallize public opinion on this subject, and, even to this day, constitute unforgotten cornerstones of industrial liberty.

LOEWE THE HATTER

The clock of industrial events was about to strike the hour. Boycotting was increasing, the boycotters refused to desist. The American Anti-Boycott Association had been organized and had declared they must desist. The public had become interested. It was time for D. E. Loewe, the Danbury hatter and the latest victim, to walk upon the stage. It was time for the famous Danbury Hatters' case to test the legality of interstate boycotting.

The attack of the Hatters' Union and the American Federation of Labor on D. E. Loewe

& Company, a small manufacturer at Danbury, Connecticut, was unprovoked. Mr. Loewe had risen from the ranks, knew his men familiarly, and employed union and non-union men without discrimination. Half of his eligible employes were members of the Hatters' Union but he refused to dismiss his loyal non-union employes. He had an untarnished record. He shunned publicity, bravado, and invectives and could not be pictured as a harsh or rabid employer. During the protracted battle, which made him a target, out of the hundreds of employes and customers with whom he had years of dealing, none were found to say aught against him. His assailants, on the other hand, were bold and ruthless; their power and resources were great. Up to this time, impunity had been their principal instructor.

The unions could not have picked a worse case upon which to stake the issue. The employers could not have chosen more wisely. Years afterwards a Connecticut jury, deliberating on the facts with the spirit of the evangelist, awarded the plaintiff the full amount sought although the claim was for prospective profits incapable of exact measurement, and rose to sing the Doxology at the close of its deliberations.

The deliberate and unprovoked aggression

THE ATTACK ON LOEWE

of the unions is shown by the order of events. In 1898 all but about a dozen of the hat manufacturers had been forced to unionize. In 1900 the Hatters' Union made application to the American Federation of Labor to boycott the concern of F. Berg and Company of Orange, New Jersey. That fight lasted eleven months, when the company surrendered. It cost the union $18,000. Then followed an attack in April, 1901, against Henry H. Roelofs & Company of Philadelphia which lasted fourteen months, and cost the union over $20,000. Roelofs succumbed on the 19th of July, 1902. Less than a week later the national officers of the Hatters' Union were in Danbury, making their final demands on D. E. Loewe & Company. They told Mr. Loewe that they had spent large sums of money in unionizing Berg and Roelofs, and, if he was unwilling to yield to their demands, they would employ their "usual methods." Thus the fight started. In order to be fair to the members of the union, Mr. Loewe published in the local newspapers and mailed to individual hatters in the summer of 1902, a warning to the effect that, if the attack continued, they would be liable. But of no avail. Loewe was put on the unfair list of the American Federation of Labor. Shipments were traced by spies. Central trades councils in towns where customers were located were wired to prevent the customers even receiving the goods already en route. Active boycotting operations were directed against loyal customers in Philadelphia, Chicago, Boston, Richmond, Omaha, Georgia, Alabama, Minnesota, Nebraska and many other places. Union agents were sent to the Pacific coast to destroy the business of the commission house of Trieste and Company, the most important customer. Shipments of Trieste and Company were traced from Seattle to San Diego, and back into Utah, and wholesalers and retailers purchasing goods from Trieste were boycotted. Throughout the entire length of the Pacific coast, every state federation, substantially every trades council. and some 2,000 local unions participated in these activities. Referring to the fight being carried on, an agent of the Hatters' Union declared to one dealer: "They had $100,000 to do it, and did not care whether it took one or two or three years. They had already beaten the firm of F. Berg & Company and Henry H. Roelofs & Company, and they did not think they would have such a hard time beating Loewe or Trieste & Company." Years after, Mr. Merritt as one of Loewe's counsel retraced these steps in taking depositions to prove these activities.

**DANBURY
HATTERS' CASE
STARTED**

To meet this attack, and recover damages for the losses inflicted, the Danbury Hatters case was instituted about Labor Day, 1903, in the District Court of the United States for the District of Connecticut—a federal suit under the Sherman Anti-Trust Law against 240 members of the Hatters' Union, to recover treble damages in the amount of $240,000. At the same time, as an anchor to windward, a corresponding suit was brought in the state court to be used as a last resort in the event that the federal suit failed. It was difficult even to secure the printing of the voluminous complaints, as the printer feared union interference, but the papers were finally printed, and the marshal and sheriff began their rounds, serving the writs which attached homes and bank accounts in Danbury, Bethel, and Norwalk.

The institution of these damage suits had some moral effect, but did not stop the attack on the Pacific Coast. Two years later, and while the damage cases were still in their indeterminate stages, it was necessary for Mr. Loewe to cross the continent to San Francisco in order to obtain a federal injunction.

The barest outline of the federal suit indicates the tortuous course it followed through the courts. After going through many preliminary steps in the lower courts, it finally reached the Supreme Court of the United States on demurrer. On February 3, 1908, that court rendered the all-important decision that the Anti-Trust Law prohibited any combination in interstate commerce which restricted "the liberty of a trader to engage in business." The claim of the labor organizations that only those engaged in commerce could restrain commerce, and that unions could therefor interrupt commerce with impunity because they were not competitors in commerce, was definitely rejected.

SUPREME COURT DECISION

Thereafter the case was twice tried before a jury, and in June, 1915, defendants were asking the United States Supreme Court to reverse a final judgment for $252,300. The Supreme Court held otherwise in an opinion which declared in substance that the use of the unfair list, "irrespective of compulsion or even an agreement to observe its intimation", if intended to restrain commerce among the states, constituted a violation of the Sherman Anti-Trust Law.

During the course of the litigation, the American Federation of Labor had come to the rescue and in 1908 passed a resolution as follows: "Resolved, That, we, the American Federation of Labor, in 28th Annual Convention assembled, do hereby pledge to the United Hatters of North America, and espe-

THE A. F. OF L. TO THE DEFENSE

cially to the 250 members of that organization whose homes and bank accounts are attached, moral and such financial support as may be necessary in the pending contention."[1] Moneys were afterward collected by assessment of the membership to carry out the purposes of the resolution and the case was conducted in part at least under the direction of attorneys chosen by the Federation.

COLLECTING THE JUDGMENT

Although the litigation was in its twelfth year when final judgment was affirmed by the Supreme Court, the end was not in sight. It was necessary to collect the judgment. Suits were accordingly started against the various savings banks to recover the moneys attached. Even that suit had to go to the United States Supreme Court to settle the question whether the attachment carried with it the accumulated interest as well as the principal.

It was also necessary to foreclose judgment liens on the various pieces of real estate in Danbury, Bethel and Norwalk. Suits started for that purpose proceeded in due course. The advertisement of the sales of the various plots scheduled to take place in July, 1917, covered several pages in the local press. In all it was estimated that, pursuing the greatest diligence, it would take two weeks to complete

[1] Resolution No. 97—Report of Proceedings of the 28th Annual Convention, American Federation of Labor, November, 1908.

the numerous public auctions. The great speculation, the great trial of nerves, was whether the American Federation of Labor or the Hatters' Union would settle to save the defendants' homes from sale or whether the plaintiff would be obliged to go through the painful process of publicly selling these homes. Sensational newspapers published pictures of old men being ejected and thrown with beds and bedding into slushy streets. At the last moment a settlement was finally reached and the sale of the homes was averted by the unions coming to the rescue. Thus ended once and for all the details of the Danbury Hatters' case.

It settled two fundamental principles. It established the law that combinations of employes, themselves not engaged in interstate commerce, may not obstruct the free flow of interstate commerce or the liberty of the trader to engage therein. It was no accident or miscarriage of justice, as asserted by the unions that a law designed to protect industrial liberty should be found applicable to combinations of workers as well as owners. On the free flow of interstate commerce the public secure their sovereign right of choice as consumers. Combinations, whether of employers or employes, which aim to keep goods out of the market and out of the reach of the public militate against this public

PRINCIPLES ESTABLISHED

policy and infringe upon the fundamental right of commercial suffrage.

The other major point settled by the Hatters' case was that members of a labor union electing officers to serve them in carrying out the purposes of that union are liable for what those officers do within the scope of their employment, and particularly so when those officers have been publicly acting in such a way that the members knew, or ought to have known, what was happening.

THE SIGNIFICANCE OF THE CASE

The case might well be called a *cause celebrè*. It was fourteen years in the courts. It was twice tried by a jury, four times was it before the United States Circuit Court of Appeals on appeal, and went three times to the United States Supreme Court. Some sixty defendants died during the course of the litigation as well as many judges who participated in the case during some stage of its progress It resulted in the complete abandonment of the unfair list by the American Federation of Labor. It demonstrated the fact that the protest of the American people against combinations of this character, which had first been stimulated in 1902, was not "idle, impudent and impotent." Its result found its way into the platforms of at least one of the great political parties, and a great statesman who had formerly sat on the Supreme Court was pub-

30

licly heckled concerning it when stumping as a candidate for President. Probably no case, except the Dred Scott decision, ever caused greater agitation in legal and political circles, and few, if any, have exercised greater influence on our industrial institutions. It forbade that the closed shop be forced by interstate boycotts.

The money collected in the Hatters' case was all turned over to Mr. Loewe without deduction for the enormous disbursements made in the conduct of the case. The payment made it possible for Loewe to continue business. American Industry, and particularly the members of the American Anti-Boycott Association, were amply rewarded by the principles established and the protection afforded.

To Daniel Davenport is due the major credit for this great case. The creative work, starting with the conception of the case, and the drafting of a masterful complaint, and the unfailing confidence that the legal trail being blazed was legally straight, were all his. Others may have helped in the presentation and prosecution of the case during its various stages, but the genius of leadership and originality was his.

During the early progress of the Hatters' case another drama of national importance **EXCITED DISCUSSION** had begun. Mr. C. W. Post, of Postum and Grape Nut fame, started a campaign for the organization of local associations throughout the country to be federated as a "Citizens' Industrial Alliance," and promoted it by anti-union utterances of such a vigorous character that his name became a by-word in labor union circles. At the same time, David M. Parry, as president of the National Association of Manufacturers, the largest employers' association in the United States, took a similar position, and became a prominent figure in the campaign to resist union encroachments. In 1906, Mr. James W. Van Cleave, president of the Buck's Stove and Range Company, of St. Louis, succeeded Mr. Parry, and with unabated vehemence carried forward a similar line of propaganda. The utterances of this so-called "Parry-Post-Van Cleave Combine" which, to labor leaders, personified the forces of wealth opposed to unions and the utterances of labor leaders on the other side painted the background of an intense, interesting and unique struggle, when human feeling ran high and prejudices often paralyzed reason. It brought into prominence all pending labor litigation, which included two of the most important cases in the history of our country.

Perhaps the utterance which most disturbed the Federation and Mr. Gompers was that made by Mr. Van Cleave in the year 1907 when he recommended a federation of the employers of the country and the raising of $500,000 a year for three years to "free this country from industrial oppression." Mr. Gompers countered in an editorial captioned, "Capitalists' War Fund to Crush Labor."[1]

In a following issue of the "Federationist" he declared "the hide-bound Van Cleave-Parry-Post aggregation may well go to, with their antiquated methods and picayunish $1,500,000 'war fund.' Organized labor is here to stay!"[2] In January, 1908, he added "Van Cleave's reptile hirelings may spend the $1,500,000 war fund in the campaign of character assassination, but it will be in vain."[3]

Editorials in the "Federationist" were also bitterly attacking injunctions. Bills were being pressed in Congress to abolish injunctions. The courts of Illinois and Massachusetts and certain individual judges were particularly under fire, and Mr. Taft, whom Mr. Gompers refers to as then being a Presidential aspirant, was criticized as an injunction judge and an ally of Van Cleave.

Thus the issue was framed. Thus the standard bearers of both sides were adding

[1] American Federationist, July, 1907, p. 476.
[2]   "   "   September, 1907, p. 677.
[3]   "   "   January, 1908, p. 27.

33

fuel to the flames, and bitterness and personalities were injected into fundamental issues of opposing philosophical thought in a way that was all together undesirable.

BUCK'S STOVE AND RANGE CO.

In the meanwhile, the Buck's Stove and Range Company in its factories at St. Louis had difficulty with the International Brotherhood of Foundry Employees, which led to a strike. The company was put on the unfair list of the American Federation of Labor, and an active boycott intensified by the bitterness which its president Mr. Van Cleave and the National Association of Manufacturers had inspired in the ranks of organized labor, was conducted against its products through the affiliated unions in various parts of the country. There had been an abundance of brave words on both sides. It was conceded that the time for a real test of strength was at hand.

THE A. F. OF L. SUED

In December, 1906, Mr. Van Cleave made application to the American Anti-Boycott Association for legal protection. The case was taken under advisement, developments were carefully observed, and it was finally decided to commence suit in the United States District Court for the District of Columbia. On August 19th, when the Executive Council of the American Federation of Labor was in session at Washington, D. C., the papers in the action were served on the American Federation of Labor, Mr. Gompers, its president; Frank Morrison, its secretary; John B. Lennon, its treasurer; John Mitchell, and many others. The October, 1907, issue of the "Federationist" declared:

> "The Executive Council of the American Federation of Labor has decided to make this a test case if it possibly can be done, and, if necessary, to bring it upon appeal to the Supreme Court of the United States. Of course, it is well known that the National Association of Manufacturers and the so-called Citizens' Industrial Alliance (of both of which Mr. Van Cleave is president, as well as being president of the Buck's Stove and Range Co.) have raised a war fund of $500,000 for this year, and propose to raise another million dollars within the coming two years to crush organized labor." (pp. 784-5.)

The American Federation of Labor immediately emulated the National Association of Manufacturers, and issued an appeal to all organized labor and friends of justice for contributions so that a "legal defense fund may be at the disposal of the American Federation of Labor to defend the rights of labor and the rights of our people before the courts."

The October, 1907, "Federationist" had much more to say about this event:

"When Mr. Van Cleave recommended to the National Association of Manufacturers the creation of this fund, and the convention of the Association adopted the policy, we pointed this out. How much of the $500,000 available for this year's campaign of 'education' by the manufacturers' association is to be utilized in its suit against the Executive Council of the American Federation of Labor we are not certain, but this we do know, that long after the Van Cleave war fund has been exhausted, and the ignorant, hostile National Association of Manufacturers has gone out of existence, labor will give its patronage to its friends and withhold it from its enemies."[1]

Another editorial asserted:

"Until a law is passed making it compulsory upon labor men to buy Van Cleave's stoves, we need not buy them, we won't buy them, and we will persuade other fair-minded sympathetic friends to co-operate with us and leave the blame things alone.

"Go to —— with your injunctions. * * *

"The Buck's Stove and Range Company of St. Louis (of which Mr. Van Cleave is president), will continue to be regarded and treated as unfair until it comes to an honorable agreement with organized labor. And this, too, whether or not it appears on the 'we don't patronize' list."[2]

[1] American Federationist, October, 1907, p. 785.
[2]   "   "   "   1907, p. 792.

In his Labor Day speech, at the Jamestown Exposition, that same year, Mr. Gompers referred to this matter, saying:

"I desire it to be clearly understood that when any court undertakes, without warrant of law, by the injunction process, to deprive me of my personal rights and my personal liberty guaranteed by the Constitution, I shall have no hesitancy in asserting and exercising those rights. And it may not be amiss to sound a word of warning and advice to such of the rampant, vindictive, greedy employers, who seek to rob the working people of our country of their lawful and constitutional rights by the unwarranted injunction process."[1]

Much of this talk on the part of the "Federationist" was far away from the facts. Neither the National Association of Manufacturers nor the Citizens' Industrial Alliance ever had anything to do with the commencement or conduct of the Buck's Stove and Range Company case or of the contempt proceedings which followed hard upon it. Not a penny of the so-called fund of $500,000 to be raised by the National Association, if it ever were raised, ever went to support this litigation. The entire direction of the case and its entire financial support fell upon the American Anti-Boycott Association, of which Mr. Van

---

[1] American Federationist, October, 1907, p. 789.

Cleave was a member. The fact, however, that Mr. Van Cleave was so intimately connected with these other associations and had become such an outspoken leader in opposition to these practices of labor unions did tend to give this case a picturesqueness and prominence which it otherwise might not have received. The unions made the National Association of Manufacturers the target of abuse, while the taciturn American Anti-Boycott Association, which in fact shouldered the entire responsibility, remained in the background.

**THE BOYCOTT
ENJOINED**

After the application for a preliminary injunction had been heard, Justice Ashley M. Gould of the Supreme Court of the District of Columbia granted an injunction on December 18, 1907, subject to the proviso that the complainant should first execute a bond. In the meanwhile, between the date of the order and the filing of the bond, the "Federationist" "rushed" the publication and circulation of its January issue still containing the name of the Buck's Stove and Range Company on its unfair list in order to anticipate the effective date of the injunction. In that way, it was hoped to circumvent the injunction without being technically guilty of a violation. The January issue thus found its way to the public unchanged, but it was the last issue ever to carry the name of the Buck's Stove and Range Company as "unfair."

The trial of the Buck's Stove and Range Company case proceeded with unusual promptness, and a final decree was entered on March 23, 1908. In the meanwhile, except for discontinuing the unfair list, the defendants seemed unimpressed with the need for discretion or restraint. They were obviously determined to trifle with the law, and as far as possible to exasperate counsel and the courts.

FLOUTING THE INJUNCTION

At the annual convention of the United Mine Workers, held January 5, 1908, with John Mitchell in the chair, a resolution was passed:

> "Resolved, That the United Mine Workers of America, in Nineteenth Annual Convention assembled, place the Buck's stoves and ranges on the unfair list, and any member of the U. M. W. of A. purchasing a stove of above make be fined $5.00, and, failing to pay the same, be expelled from the organization."

That resolution was likewise published in the United Mine Workers Journal.

"All the Justice Goulds, Buck's Stove and Range Company injunctions and the United States Supreme Court Judges will some day be in Heaven or H—— and trade unionism will still flourish, so don't worry," declared another Union periodical. Mr. Gompers, in an address in New York said: "I want to say this about that, injunction or no injunction, I won't buy a Loewe hat nor a Buck stove or range." In another address, May, 1908, repeating the same suggestions, he added: "And, by the way, I don't know why you should buy any of that sort of stuff. I won't; but that is a matter to which we can refer more particularly in our organizations."

FIRST CONTEMPT PROCEEDING

Because of these insidious speeches and editorials, Samuel Gompers, John Mitchell and Frank Morrison were found guilty of contempt of court by Judge Wright on December 23rd, 1908, and sentenced to jail respectively for twelve months, nine months and six months.

The defendants appealed the case involving the permanent injunction and also the contempt cases, to the Court of Appeals of the District of Columbia. On March 11, 1909, the Court of Appeals sustained the injunction, in modified form, and on November 2, 1909, the sentences for contempt were sustained. Both cases then landed where both parties wanted them to land—in the United States Supreme Court. The final goal was at hand. The Supreme Court would dispose of the issues.

THE COMPANY SURRENDERS

Mr. Van Cleave died unexpectedly in May,

1910, and the management of the Buck's Stove and Range Company fell into the hands of Mr. Fred W. Gardiner, the largest stockholder. He was a man of different type from Mr. Van Cleave. One imagines he always proceeded quietly and adroitly to avoid issues. Mr. Van Cleave was of the type which ran up the flag and with trumpets sounding prepared to go to the stake. Mr. Gardiner, as he subsequently stated, had not approved of Mr. Van Cleave's attitude on the labor question, and accordingly, when the change took place, he determined that the Buck's Stove and Range Company should be regarded as a friend of the American Federation of Labor, and proceeded to take all steps necessary to attain that end. Just when he first approached the officials of the American Federation of Labor for a settlement is not known, but it was always suspected that he did so before he consulted his counsel or the American Anti-Boycott Association. On June 15, 1910, at his own solicitation, he attended a meeting of the General Executive Board of the American Anti-Boycott Association, and presented figures showing, as he claimed, the extent to which his business had been injured by the boycott. The figures did show a falling off of forty per cent of his business due to some cause. Mr. Gardiner spoke of a possible receivership, and declared that now Mr. Van Cleave was dead he wished to settle the case and to secure a letter from Mr. Gompers that hostilities had ceased and his concern was in favor of the American Federation of Labor.

No decision was reached at that meeting, but Mr. Gardiner was informed that, while the suit for the injunction could be settled, it was otherwise with the contempt proceedings because the court had become an interested party.

TERMS OF SURRENDER   Mr. Gardiner made his peace with Mr. Gompers. On July 19, 1910, in Cincinnati, the Buck's Stove and Range Company, and the various unions, executed a written agreement which provided:

> "That the labor organizations in interest herein named shall jointly make known and publicly declare that all controversy or difference with the Buck's Stove and Range Company of St. Louis has been satisfactorily and honorably adjusted.

> "That the Buck's Stove and Range Company through its representatives * * * agree that it will withdraw its attorneys from any case pending in the courts, which have grown out of the dispute between the American Federation of Labor, and any of its affiliated organizations on the one hand, and the Buck's Stove and Range

Company on the other, and that the said Company will not bring any proceedings in the courts against an individual or organizations growing out of any past controversies between said Company and organized labor. * * *

"And as far as practical, every publicity be given to the satisfactory agreement reached between the Buck's Stove and Range Company and the American Federation of Labor."[1]

Headquarters of the
AMERICAN FEDERATION OF LABOR
Washington, D. C.
July 29, 1910.

TO ALL WHOM IT MAY CONCERN:

An honorable agreement has been reached between the Buck's Stove and Range Company and the American Federation of Labor and its affiliated organizations primarily interested.

The long drawn out industrial dispute has been adjusted.

The new mangement of the Buck's Stove and Range Company has always been, is now, and proposes to continue friendly to organized labor.

Labor in its struggle for the workers' rights earnestly seeks agreements with employers who are fair-minded, and fair

---

[1] American Federationist, September, 1910, p. 808.

in their attitude toward and dealings with organized labor. Such is the position of the Buck's Stove and Range Company and the American Federation of Labor. The Company is now entitled to, and should receive, the courtesy, consideration, and patronage which Labor, its friends and sympathizers can give it.

Secretaries are requested to read this notice at the meetings of their respective organizations and labor and reform press please copy."[1]

"And thus ends," says the "Federationist," "one of the most noted industrial disputes in the history of labor."[2]

Of course Mr. Gompers hailed the outcome as a great victory and as further evidence of the invincibility of labor:

"That it will have a tendency to have employers generally come into more agreement with organized labor there can be no question. The agreement with the Buck's Stove and Range Company and organized labor will have far-reaching influence upon the progress and success in the evolutionary development of the movement of our country and contribute much to the common uplift of all labor, of all our people."[3]

Mr. C. W. Post, an important stockholder in the Buck's Stove and Range Company op-

[1] American Federationist, September, 1910, p. 760.
[2] "   "   "   1910, p. 808.
[3] "   "   "   1910, p. 812.

posed this settlement from the outset, and his personal influence being unavailing endeavored to secure an injunction against the carrying out of this agreement which he alleged to be illegal. When he failed in that suit, he instituted a proceeding, as a minority stockholder, to compel the company to prosecute a damage suit for $750,000, under the Sherman Anti-Trust Law. This also come to naught. The fight between the Buck's Stove and Range Company and the American Federation of Labor was at an end.

The chapter on legal events, at least so far as it related to the contempt proceeding, was not so easily closed. When the pending appeals came before the United States Supreme Court, the first case to be considered was the appeal in relation to the injunction suit. As that case was called for argument, one of the justices leaned forward and asked if the rumors concerning a settlement of this case had any foundation, and being told that they had, the case was treated as a moot case and the appeal dismissed.

IN THE UNITED STATES SUPREME COURT

With the contempt cases, the course of events was different. The Court heard the arguments and on May 15, 1911, rendered a decision reversing the sentences on the theory that the contempts were of a criminal nature while the proceeding on its face bore all the indicia of a civil proceeding. Under such circumstances, the Court held the defendants had not been properly warned by the nature of the proceeding that they might be jailed for criminal contempt. The case was then remanded to the lower court "but without prejudice to the power and right of the Supreme Court of the District of Columbia, to punish by a proper proceeding, contempt, if any, committed against it."

THE DECISION

The decision of the Supreme Court, however, established the underlying principles of the illegality of the boycott, and the power of the court to enjoin it. The defendants' major contention, that such an injunction offended the constitutional provisions protecting freedom of press and speech was repudiated. In the Hatters' case the court had already reaffirmed the doctrine that no means, however innocent or constitutionally protected, can be employed in furtherance of illegal schemes, and it was only necessary to reassert this doctrine in other language, which declared:

"The court's protective and restraining powers extend to every device whereby property is irreparably damaged or commerce is illegally restrained."

The court then came to that ever-embarrassing question of the proper adjustment be-

tween social or associated action on the one
hand, and the proper protection of the non-
conformist individual on the other:

> "Society itself is an organization and
> does not object to organizations for so-
> cial, religious, business and all legal pur-
> poses. The law, therefore, recognizes the
> right of workingmen to unite and to in-
> vite others to join their ranks, thereby
> making available the strength, influence
> and power that come from such associa-
> tion. By virtue of this right, powerful
> labor unions have been organized.

**INDIVIDUALISM
VS.
COLLECTIVISM**

> "But the very fact that it is lawful to
> form these bodies, with multitudes of
> members, means that they have thereby
> acquired a vast power, in the presence of
> which the individual may be helpless.
> This power, when unlawfully used against
> one, cannot be met, except by his pur-
> chasing peace at the cost of submitting
> to terms which involve the sacrifice of
> rights protected by the Constitution; or
> by standing on such rights and appealing
> to the preventive powers of a court of
> equity. When such appeal is made, it is
> the duty of government to protect the
> one against the many, as well as the many
> against the one."[1]

The power of the courts to punish for contempt for violation of its orders was upheld in
no uncertain terms:

---

[1] Gompers vs. Buck's Stove and Range Co., 221 U. S. 418.

"And, if upon the examination of the record it should appear that the defendants were in fact and in law guilty of the contempt charged, there could be no more important duty than to render such a decree as would serve to vindicate the jurisdiction and authority of courts to enforce orders and to punish acts of disobedience. For while it is sparingly to be used, yet the power of courts to punish for contempts is a necessary and integral part of the independence of the judiciary, and is absolutely essential to the performance of the duties imposed on them by law. Without it they are mere boards of arbitration whose judgments and decrees would be only advisory."[1]

So the labor leaders were discharged on technical grounds of procedure but the principle objective, which was to establish the law for the benefit of all so that business could secure prompt relief in the lower courts, was won. The equity powers of the courts to enjoin boycotts, no matter if carried on by human speech, and to thus protect the liberty of employers to conduct their business as they see fit, was thus well grounded.

SECOND CONTEMPT PROCEEDING

The following day, the Supreme Court of the District of Columbia, acting on the remanding order of the United States Supreme Court, appointed a committee to inquire whether there was reasonable cause to believe that Messrs. Gompers, Mitchell and Morrison

[1] Gompers vs. Buck's Stove and Range Co., 221 U. S. 418.

had been guilty of wilfully violating an injunction order of the court. On June 26th, 1911, the committee reported that these three persons were guilty of specific acts in violation of the outstanding injunction. A trial took place in which the defendants set up the statute of limitations as a defense. On appeal to the District Court of Appeals, modified sentences were affirmed. The case then came again before the United States Supreme Court, and on May 11, 1914, an opinion was rendered by Mr. Justice Holmes reversing the sentences and holding that the statute of limitations "which is their only real defense" was a bar to the second proceeding by the District Court. It was a curious outcome. The Supreme Court, on May 15, 1911, had reversed the first contempt proceedings without prejudice to the right of the Supreme Court of the District of Columbia to start further proceeding, and, when on the following day the Supreme Court of the District of Columbia acted on this suggestion, the Supreme Court of the United States on final appeal held that the statute of limitations had already run against further proceedings.

THE STATUTE OF LIMITATIONS

So ended the boycott conducted on a national scale by the American Federation of Labor. In its old form, it has never been revived. Efforts to change the law as laid down

THE BOYCOTT RETIRED

in these two cases proved unavailing. The so-
called bill of rights in the Clayton Act of 1914,
of which we shall speak later, failed to accomplish the desired result. The law of the Hatters' case and the law of the Buck's Stove and
Range Company case still remain the law of
the land after many years of political and legal
contest.

After all the boasting and speechmaking
with which this contest commenced, and after
the smoke of actual battle had cleared away, a
simple chronology tells the tale. The bond to
make effective the injunction of the Buck's
Stove and Range Company was effective December 23rd, 1907. After January, 1908, the
Buck's name disappeared from the unfair list.
On February 3rd, 1908, the Supreme Court
rendered its first decision in the Hatters' case.
In March, 1908, the unfair list of the Federation ceased to exist. Mr. Gompers explained
this action to the readers of the "Federationist" by announcing that the publication of the
unfair list "makes the organization and the individuals composing it liable to monetary
damages and imprisonment. * * * This being
the case I feel obliged to discontinue the 'We
don't patronize' list." And he added, "Labor
demands relief at the hands of Congress; demands it **NOW**."[1]

---

[1] American Federationist, March, 1908, p. 192.

Of the legal principles at issue, the Federation lost all. It had to abandon the boycott. As to fatalities, the score was more evenly balanced. The labor leaders did not go to jail and the Buck's Stove and Range Company lowered its colors. But Loewe, the hatter, still makes open shop hats and people buy them.

NET RESULTS

In the meanwhile a new kind of boycotting machinery of an equally menacing character was being forged. The 1906 Convention of the American Federation of Labor, declaring that the Manufacturers' Association and the Building Trades Employers' Association were endeavoring to destroy the building trades in Pittsburgh, passed a resolution authorizing the president "to call a meeting of all representatives of building trades organizations to meet at a given date in the City of Pittsburg to devise ways and means of overcoming this desperate battle."[1] That meeting was held in 1907, and resulted in the establishment of the Building Trades Department of the American Federation of Labor, representing the various building trades unions with a total membership of about half a million.

THE BUILDING TRADES

The 1907 convention of the Federation also voted to create and charter a Metal Trades

---

[1] Report of Proceedings of the 26th Annual Convention of the American Federation of Labor, 1906, p. 143.

Department. It included sheet metal workers, machinists, electricians, steam fitters and other organizations, having a total membership of about 230,000.

Reporting on the Building Trades Department in June, 1909, the "American Federationist" declared:

> "No other agency can compare with it in directness and efficiency in the fight for better conditions and the thorough unionizing of the allied crafts. * * * With every trade employed upon a building, from the turning of the first spadeful of earth until the window shades are in position, standing shoulder to shoulder, a solid unit, each refusing to turn a hand until the contract for every hour's labor on the job has been let to a fair firm—the owner and the contractor must do business with our organization."[1]

THE METAL TRADES DEPARTMENT A. F. OF L.

The Metal Trades Department, at its convention in 1910, declared that the Department was not as yet so far perfected as to "make it compulsory for affiliated organizations to order their members on strike in sympathy or otherwise at the whim or call of an affiliated organization whose grievance may be real or imaginary." At the same convention a resolution was introduced instructing the incoming Executive Board "to meet the Executive

---

[1] American Federationist, June, 1909, pp. 526-7.

Board of the Building Trades Department and other departments to the end of securing the co-operation of the Building Trades Department in refusing to handle the product of firms against whom the metal trades have strikes." This resolution was objected to on the ground that it was limited to unfair products where strikes had occurred, and a more general resolution was substituted for a conference between the departments "to the end of securing the co-operation of these departments for our mutual advancement." In the latter part of 1910, Albert J. Berres, secretary of the Metal Trades Department, addressed a convention of the Building Trades Department, and said: "Heretofore very little consideration has been given by the building trades men as to how the machinery and the general supplies for their work have been manufactured." He suggested that they take the position "that unless it was manufactured under fair conditions they could not handle it." And added, "We have to resort to all sorts of things to compete with the captains of industry."

The Executive Council of the same building trades convention urged further negotiations with the Metal Trades Department "with a view to unionizing such work in the metal industry as comes in contact with building erection," and recommended further co-operation "with a view to having machinery used in the buildings made under fair conditions, and with a further view to assisting the Metal Trades Department when machinery coming from unfair shops is being put into buildings."

TO STRIKE AGAINST OPEN SHOP MATERIALS

An organization was thus built, which, if successfully operated, according to the purpose of its creators, provided for strikes of all trades on any building where so-called "unfair materials" or "unfair machinery" was being used. Its first operation was against the manufacturers of refrigerating machinery. The Metal Trades Department, failing to secure a union agreement with a large manufacturer of refrigerating machines, issued notices in accordance with the instructions of its board to "our local councils and all other localities where our Internationals have locals, that, where the product of this firm had been contracted for, that the members of the metal trades refuse to erect or install the same in the buildings where the machine is to go. * * * You are, therefore, requested to appoint a committee to wait on the officials of ———— (naming a customer) and notify them that union labor will refuse to install said machines until such time as an agreement is reached between ———— company and this Department. You will be informed from time to time when new contracts are let for the product of this firm and by whom."

This new form of boycott had been highly developed by the Carpenters' Union, the second most powerful trade union in the United States, and a few other national unions. In New York City it was successful in excluding practically all doors, sash or wood trim produced by open shop manufacturers in spite of the fact that these open shop products could be purchased for twenty-five percent less than the union products. The local union manufacturers worked in close co-operation with the union, and at times employed spies to discover importations of open shop products. The buildings were then tied up by a strike. So tight was this monopoly that open shop manufacturers in Brooklyn could not ship their product into Manhattan, and inter-borough trade was impossible. The city was as completely shut off from the benefits of open shop competition as if it had been surrounded by a Chinese wall.

CARPENTERS' UNION

The first suit to test this question was brought in the Federal Court in behalf of Irving & Casson of Boston, a member of the American Anti-Boycott Association. Because this open shop concern was making the choir stall for the Cathedral of St. John the Divine, the unions threatened to tie up the

WOOD TRIM FROM OPEN SHOPS

whole enterprise "as tight as a drum." An injunction saved the day but the union wisely enough did not appeal the case.

During the same year, a group of large open shop manufacturers of these products, located in Wisconsin, Iowa, Pennsylvania and Tennessee, came to the American Anti-Boycott Association to test the legality of such operations and action was commenced in the Federal Courts. The lower court granted a preliminary injunction, but, when the case came on for final hearing, the same court—and subsequently the Circuit Court of Appeals—held that a private party was not entitled to an injunction under the federal anti-trust law, that remedy being reserved to the Attorney General. And so the case arrived in the Supreme Court of the United States, where it proved a perplexing one. It was first argued in May, 1915, and about a year later, on the initiative of the court, was restored to the docket for reargument. In the meanwhile, Mr. Justice Hughes had retired to run for the Presidency, and Justice Clarke had been appointed to succeed him. The case was finally reargued in October, 1916, and decided June 11, 1917, by a divided court of five to four. In a short memorandum, five of the judges held that a private party was not entitled to an injunction under the anti-trust law. Justice Pitney, writing a long and thorough opinion, which it was generally suspected was originally the majority opinion, declared that there was no difference between the members of the court on the question as to whether the combination violated the Sherman Anti-Trust Law, but only on the question as to whether a private party was entitled to an injunction under that law. Thus, while this case was technically lost, it practically constituted another victory for the cause of industrial liberty. It strengthened the claim that combinations of that character violated the anti-trust law while in the meanwhile the Clayton Act, enacted in October, 1914, cured the other difficulty by expressly declaring that a private party was entitled to an injunction.

In the courts of the State of New York the unions won a real victory. The injunctions against the Carpenters' Union were set aside by the highest court of the State and it was held that such activities violated no state law. In New York State relief could only be obtained in the federal tribunals. In other states the courts ruled otherwise. **NEW YORK DECISIONS**

Subsequently the New York State decision was considerably qualified by the case of the Auburn Draying Company, also handled by the League, where the court held that a combination of labor unions not to handle goods hauled by an open shop truckman was illegal.[1]

The federal decisions, and others which followed upon them had to some extent the same effect on this type of boycott that the Hatters' case and Buck's case had upon the other type of boycott. The program had been laid out by the Building Trades and Metal Trades Departments of the American Federation of Labor, representing three-quarters of a million mechanics to carry on sympathetic strikes of this kind for the purpose of compelling the unionization of factories. The heart was taken out of this program by legal developments, and it proved largely abortive.

PROSECUTING THE A. A. B. A.

But the way of the crusader is not usually free from counter charges and recriminations. On January 15, 1916, Henry A. Potter, Treasurer; Herman F. Lee, Secretary, and Walter Gordon Merritt, Associate Counsel, were arrested, and the American Anti-Boycott Association was summoned to appear before the Magistrate's Court in Brooklyn. When the Marshal appeared in Mr. Merritt's office and told him he was under arrest, Mr. Merritt inquired, "What for?" The officer said, "For practicing law and giving legal advice." Mr. Merritt's rejoinder was, "What do you suppose I studied law for?" The officer laughed,

[1]Auburn Draying Co., *v.* Wardell, 227 N. Y.

58

and said the whole matter was a mystery to him, and exhibited the warrant which stated the charge as "unlawfully practicing law and giving legal advice." Of course the parties hied to the Magistrate's Court. There the defendants waived examination, and the case was held for Special Sessions.

The newspapers proclaimed the event with headlines, "Labor Hits at Its Old Foe." The labor unions felt confident that this would be an end of organized effort to enforce the law against their illegal practices, and their feelings found expression in another headline, "Labor Leaders See End of Opposition in Court Decision." The union's attorneys declared: "This is the beginning of the end of the Anti-Boycott Association. It has operated against labor unions for fifteen years, and we will show that it is nothing more than a corporation of lawyers." Mr. Beattie, the union's attorney, declared: "Labor unions having come to the conclusion that it was time for the worm to turn, and prevent what they call a blind pool to fight labor, decided on the present criminal proceeding." Mr. Merritt declared: "The American Anti-Boycott Association is a public spirited organization, formed to establish industrial peace and justice, and is now attacked by the Carpenters' Union on the ground that it furnishes counsel to secure protection for its members against criminal conspiracies of labor."

PRACTISING LAW?

What was it all about? Since 1909, Section 280 of the Penal Law had forbidden corporations to practice or appear as an attorney or to hold itself out as entitled to practice law or furnish legal advice, with a maximum penalty of a year's imprisonment and $1,000 fine. In 1911 this law was amended so that its prohibitions extended to voluntary associations. This extension was enacted largely at the instance of certain mercantile interests to reach collection agencies which were evading the law relative to corporations by practicing law as voluntary associations. The Carpenters' Union also claimed credit for the change. When Mr. John Kirby, president of the National Association of Manufacturers, was in the Canadian woods he met the attorney for the carpenters, who in a moment of indiscretion, boasted that the union had secured this change of the law in order to prosecute the American Anti-Boycott Association and its officers.

Whichever was the greater influence in securing the enactment of this law, there was no doubt as to the origin and instigation of the prosecution against the Association. An affidavit filed by Otto A. Gillig, a young man associated with Mr. Beattie, charged the Association and its counsel, Mr. Merritt, with starting and maintaining practically a dozen different suits against the Carpenters' Union in the City of New York as well as a suit against the photoengravers, and prayed "that the defendants be apprehended and dealt with according to law." The case came on for trial November 15, 1916, before three judges sitting in Special Sessions, Second Division, Brooklyn. After the evidence was taken, the defendants giving a full, frank, and clear statement of its purposes and activities, the court dismissed the case, one judge dissenting.

In the meanwhile the District Council of Carpenters commenced suit in November, 1911, to enjoin the American Anti-Boycott Association from continuing its court activities, and the Association employed Hon. Charles E. Littlefield, formerly Congressman from Maine, to defend.

ENJOINING THE A. A. B. A?

The complaint alleged that the Association had raised "vast sums of money" to carry on litigation against labor organizations and had conspired against the Joint District Council by authorizing Walter Gordon Merritt, its salaried officer and attorney, to act for members in suits against the carpenters. The object of the Association in such litigation, it was alleged, "is to harass and destroy said Joint District Council, and to impoverish it."

The first application for a preliminary injunction was dismissed without prejudice. On the second, Judge Bijur, of the Supreme Court of the State of New York, held on March 23, 1912, "I do not think that the defendant Association is shown to violate either the letter or the spirit of Section 280 of the Penal Law." The case dragged on until the end of the year, when on final trial Justice Ford held "that the defendant's activities transgressed the statute in question seems quite clear." He found, however, that the Carpenters' Union had no standing in court to secure an injunction because it was merely seeking by indirection to enforce a criminal law. The case was accordingly dismissed. Subsequent efforts by the plaintiff to alter this decision by appeal proved unavailing.

In the summer of 1912, the carpenters pursued another ingenious course. Up to that time they had been unsuccessful in securing any court decision stopping the activities of the American Anti-Boycott Association. In order to secure a favorable decision without opposition it applied to the Appellate Division of the Supreme Court, without notice to anybody, for a ruling as to whether the union could employ an attorney to act for its members or whether such activities would violate the penal law. But the court was wary. It refused to pass upon the question, and decided that when the Carpenters' Union had completed its form of organization it would be time enough to present the question for final decision. In this way another effort to prevent the American Anti-Boycott Association from carrying on its work was frustrated.

Excitement ran high in New York City in 1912 as a result of this litigation with the Carpenters' Union. On October 26th, according to the newspapers, "an army of 25,000 belonging to the Building Trades Union, every second man carrying a small American flag, marched from Fifth Avenue and 58th Street to Cooper Union to protest against injunctions restraining union men from boycotting the use of non-union materials." They had twenty bands and there was some disorder. "The red flag," according to the union circulars, was well represented in the demonstration and the workers' 'Marseillaise' was played continuously." Inscriptions called "upon the courts to do something to wipe out the Anti-Boycott Association."

PARADES AGAINST INJUNCTIONS

When the procession arrived at Cooper Union, Eldridge H. Neal, secretary of the Carpenters' District Council, acted as chairman and Mr. Gompers was the chief speaker. The American Anti-Boycott Association was severely attacked as well as the decisions of the courts enjoining boycotting. Mr. Gompers declared, "If the judges continue to abuse the power of injunction there may be many repetitions of the Lawrence affair at Lawrence and elsewhere. We are not bound to obey an injunction in excess of the power of the Court to issue it. Men who propose to exercise the rights of American citizens must take the consequences, whatever they may be."

It was resolved "that no member of the organized mechanics of the Building Trades will hereafter work for any member of the American Anti-Boycott Association."

SCURRILOUS CIRCULARS

To add to the agitation, inflammatory circulars were distributed in New York attacking the American Anti-Boycott Association, its counsel, Mr. Merritt, and denouncing the courts:

> "It is quite clear, therefore, that if you wish to get an injunction against the workingman under similar conditions, you do not need to go to the Supreme Court, but apply to the American Anti-Boycott Association, which will prepare the papers for you and they will compel the judge to sign the paper for you. You take no risk, therefore, in employing them, for you get the injunction in any event, and the judge no longer has anything to say about it."

Judges were referred to as "little pee-wee judges * * * without a single drop of red blood" in them. It was declared that the Association had been "caught red-handed," and that the people connected with it were "criminals under the law." At the meeting of the Sixth Annual Convention of the New York State Council of Carpenters, the Committee on Legislation recommended "that the officers of this Council devote their time and money to fight the courts of our state and nation to the end that the wage earner shall have just as much right in expecting just and equitable decisions as the big interests." The national convention of carpenters declared "that the reckless and unwarranted use of court injunctions has resolved itself into mere judicial anarchy. The frightful usurpation of unwarranted power has caused hundreds of thousands of the workers and toilers of our land to be led like sheep to the shambles."

The general result of the decisions relating to strikes against non-union material was good even down to this point, but it remains to show later how completely the law resolved in favor of a free and open market for all materials. In the meanwhile we must turn to the political side of our story in order to complete the picture.

Early in the history of the American Anti-Boycott Association it became necessary to combat the efforts of organized labor to ex-   **LEGISLATION** empt more of their activities from legal restraints and responsibilities. Messrs. Daniel Davenport and James M. Beck were called upon to appear before committees in Congress in opposition to measures of this character. The first appearance received sensational recognition from the press. The "New York Sun" for April 6, 1904, declared "But this session there appeared on the scene a secret organization, the ramifications of its membership extending into all parts of the country with abundance of means to employ the best of talent and guided and directed by men of energy, purpose and force."

EXEMPTIONS FOR UNIONS

The pertinent legislative measures before Congress in these years and the following decade covered a variety of proposals. There were bills to exempt labor from the anti-trust laws, to legalize boycotting and certain other forms of conspiracy, to declare that business was not property, and, therefore, not entitled to protection in a court of equity, to abolish injunctions, to provide that injunctions should not issue without notice or hearing and that contempt proceedings for violations of injunctions should be tried by a jury. Counsel for the American Anti-Boycott Association analyzed the decisions of the Federal Courts which involved the issuance of injunctions in labor cases, and presented their analysis to Congress showing that this judicial remedy of injunction had suffered as little from indiscrete or oppressive use as any other remedy.

But the clamor for legislative relief would not down. The decisions of the courts secured by the American Anti-Boycott Association merely strengthened the union demand for legislation that would close the doors of the courts to so-called labor litigation. The utterances of organized labor were of growing intensity. "The existence of organized labor is in jeopardy," wrote the editor of the "Federationist," and "the right of free association and voluntary coalition has been denied." Other editorials were defiant and tinged with red:

> "We have steadily fought the injunction—this outrageous, impudent, revolutionary invention of lawless plutocracy—and if the national and state legislatures are reluctant or slow to come to the relief of labor and put an end by appropriate legislation to the usurpation practiced by Judges more and more audaciously at the dictation of plutocracy, other lawful ways and means of resisting the abuse will suggest themselves."[1]

Year after year committees of Congress listened to the representatives of labor unions proposing these laws, and employers' repre-

---

[1] American Federationist, April, 1906, p. 228.

sentatives and constitutional lawyers of distinction opposing them. Massive volumes now record this. The issue became of such supreme importance that it found its way into the platforms of the two great political parties. In March, 1906, the Federation and prominent national unions presented their "Bill of Grievances" to Congressmen, Senators and the President, calling for exemption from the anti-trust laws and the abolition of labor injunctions. It declared "our repeated efforts to obtain redress from Congress have been in vain."[1] It hoped their appeal would not be in vain, "But if, perchance, you may not heed us, we shall appeal to the conscience and the support of our fellow citizens."[2] A categorical answer was demanded for the purpose of definitely pledging the Congressman to the support of such measures or marking him for political slaughter at the fall elections. Answers were published in the "Federationist" and those that were "evasive or hostile or which did not harmonize with the Congressman's record were briefly commented upon by the editor," said the "Federationist." "This had the effect of convincing many that Labor's campaign was no bluff, and after that there were fewer attempts to evade or confuse the issue."[3] Answers promising to give the sub-

LABORS' BILL
OF
GRIEVANCES

---

[1] American Federationist, May, 1906, p. 295.
[2]   "   "   "   1906, p. 296.
[3]   "   "   November, 1906, p. 881.

ject "careful consideration" and to vote for the "best interests of Labor," were not satisfactory because "the gentleman seems to know better than Labor what is for their best interest." The pledge demanded of our national legislators was not only to vote for certain bills or policies, but also to accept such changes in detail as might be thereafter approved "by the legislative committee of the American Federation of Labor and the National Grange." The representatives of the people were to be rubber stamps, their functions abdicated and their duties to the general public tossed overboard. Never before was there such a public, bold and systematic attempt to lay hands on the altar of government and make it a tool for class purposes. The quiet, unseen methods of secret lobbies and boss control with which we were familiar through common gossip were less startling, if not less dangerous. "Labor's Watchword" announced:

> "We will stand by our friends and administer a stinging rebuke to men or parties who are either indifferent, negligent, or hostile, and, wherever opportunity affords, secure the election of intelligent, honest, earnest trade unionists, with clear, unblemished, paid-up union cards in their possession."[1]

[1] *American Federationist*, May, 1906, p. 319.

To realize how excessively class-conscious was this political venture, it is illuminating to follow the contemporary suggestion of one newspaper, which quoted one of Mr. Gompers' editorials after substituting the word "capital" for the word "labor":

> "The first concern of all should be the positive defeat of those who have been hostile or indifferent to the just demands of CAPITAL. A stinging rebuke to them will benefit not only the CAPITALISTS, but the people of the entire country. Wherever both parties ignore CAPITAL'S legislative demands a straight CAPITAL candidate should be nominated," etc.

HEATED CAMPAIGNS

Congressmen and Senators who were fearless and outspoken in their opposition to such legislation were attacked and this led to a personal campaign in the State of Maine by Mr. Gompers and his associates against the late Congressman Littlefield. Secretary Taft and others of national renown went to Maine and campaigned in Mr. Littlefield's behalf. "The Parry-Post-Gripe-Nuts Manufacturers' Association and so-called Citizens' Alliance," according to the Federation, "had their henchmen in the field."[1] It was a battle of national significance and Mr. Littlefield won by a greatly reduced plurality. The labor leaders

---

[1] American Federationist, October, 1906, p. 801.

were hopeful. "As Maine goes, so goes the
nation." The muse was invoked to strengthen
optimism:

> "Three cheers for Samuel Gompers,
> And long may his name wave;
> Against great odds he made a fight—it
> was a darned close shave—
> Against the greatest speakers. Adminis-
> tration gave
> One Littlefield
> Was nearly peeled
> And barely missed the grave."[1]

Attention was then turned to the coming **POLITICAL**
campaigns of Congressman McCall, "Uncle" **BLACKLIST**
Joe Cannon, Gillett, Palmer, Weeks, Gardner,
Sherman and others who were also marked
for defeat, but the results were insubstantial.
The political blacklist did not work.

Naturally labor leaders tried to convince
themselves and their followers that the campaign was a great success. Political independence and courage must not be encouraged by
the thought that there is no penalty for independent action in matters of this kind. So the
official announcement went forth:

> "Labor's political work is just begun.
> The future is ours. Labor will continue
> the work of this campaign until those who
> are hostile or negligent toward its de-
> mands are willing to accord us justice."[2]

---

[1] American Federationist, October, 1906, p. 811.
[2] "   "   December, 1906, p. 970.

Congressmen must understand why labor's initial effort did not accomplish more:

"That labor was unable to exert its entire force in the recent campaign, we frankly admit, but in spite of great difficulties it accomplished enough to give more than a hint of what it can and may do when thoroughly prepared to exercise its political strength. * * * Let no Congressman delude himself with the hope that the recent campaign was merely a spasmodic effort on the part of Labor to right its wrongs. Let no Congressman flatter himself that his future record will be concealed from the public."[1]

No such elaborate campaign on the part of the Federation was repeated after 1906, but efforts were made in subsequent elections to write labor's demands into the platforms of the political parties and to capture more Congressional seats for union men in certain promising localities. From time to time the "Federationist" reviewed the results thus attained:

"The year 1906," it said, "marked a concerted movement of organized labor into the field of national politics * * * The records of Congressmen were scrutinized * * * The first contest revealed the efficacy of the effort. Six trade unionists, in full standing with their respective organ-

<hr>

[1] American Federationist, December, 1906, p. 972.

izations, were elected to membership in the national House of Representatives."[1]

The "dominant party refused to change its policy" and organized labor proceeding with its campaign in the election of 1908 added "four additional trade unionists to the House." "Congress and the public generally became convinced that Labor proposed to exercise its political rights, to the end that Congressional relief should be secured." Labor made its third campaign in 1910, thereby "augmenting the labor group to a total of fifteen."[2]

UNION
LEGISLATORS

At the Atlantic City Convention of the American Federation of Labor in 1911, the Executive Committee was authorized "to take such action as in its judgment the situation may warrant in the presidential and congressional election of 1912."[3] The exhortation was slightly changed:

"Men of Labor, grit your teeth, organize, unite, federate. Elect bona fide trade unionists to Congress. Get busy!"[4]

The labor planks as incorporated in the national platforms were published in the Federationist and the speeches of two presidential candidates were reviewed with special emphasis on their references to the injunction.

[1] American Federationist, June, 1912, p. 459.
[2]   "   "   "   1912, p. 460.
[3]   "   "   "   1912, p. 463.
[4]   "   "   "   1912, p. 464.

The "Federationist" was careful not to dictate to its followers for whom they should vote as president, but recommended that they study the attitude of each candidate on the subject of "Relief from the Sherman Anti-Trust Law and from the issuance of Injunctions." The unionist was reminded that "the Republican candidate for the presidency being also the originator of the abuse of the injunction in labor disputes" was against any plan to weaken the courts or any form of class legislation.

In 1912 the "Federationist" summarized the situation.

> "That issue was presented in the presidential and congressional campaigns of 1908. It was an issue in the congressional campaign of 1910. It is a paramount issue in the pending presidential and congressional campaign, and, regardless of all other questions affecting the working people of the United States, all should be subordinated to the achievement of this one living, forceful issue, which the toilers and their sympathizers and all liberty-loving American citizens must determine in the election of November 5, 1912."[1]

MODEL ANTI-INJUNCTION BILL

The demands of labor unions had now become standardized. Most of them found expression in a Model Anti-Injunction Bill,

[1] American Federationist, November, 1912, p. 909.

which, in effect, declared that the right of a man to work and the right of an employer to conduct business should not be regarded as a property right entitled to protection as property in the courts of our land. These property rights were to be confiscated.

In 1913 events were imminent. The state of mind of the politician is shown by the consideration of federal appropriation bills for funds to enforce our laws, with provisos that none of the appropriated funds should be used against labor unions. Early in 1913, "after 23 years of effort, this labor proviso" says the "Federationist," "was incorporated in a bill reported from a committee." This bill was vetoed by Mr. Taft, but on June 23rd, 1913, such a bill was signed by President Wilson. "This was a decisive victory for the rights and protection of labor," wrote Mr. Gompers. A decisive victory indeed; a victory for class legislation when appropriations for the enforcement of laws provide that public funds shall not be utilized to enforce laws against some particular group! After that, President Wilson annually signed bills with similar provisos.

THE APPROPRIATION RIDER

The ground was well harrowed for the events of 1914. The Model Anti-Injunction Bill was urged for enactment before the state legislatures of our various states under a

THE CLAYTON ACT

75

nationwide campaign directed from the headquarters of the Federation at Washington. A federal bill restricting injunctions and purporting to exempt labor unions from the Anti-Trust law was ready for enactment. Hearings were shut off. The stage was well set. Labor leaders sat in the galleries during the critical sessions of Congress and their presence had its effect. The scene in the Senate was portrayed, as the Federation saw it and felt it:

> "The scene in the Senate on September 2 was intensely interesting. The day was very hot but the air was vibrant with the tenseness of the concentrated interest and earnestness of those men engaged in legislative deliberations. The quiet acceptance of Labor's contentions was very suggestive."[1]

The Clayton Act passed. "After 24 years the organizations of labor have freed themselves from this strange entanglement." The Federation contended that unions did not need the law. Unlike the captains of industry, they were not governed "by the same freebooting standards of ethics as the pirates of old." The words of the new law "are sledgehammer blows to the wrongs and injustice so long inflicted upon the workers." The long-heralded declaration, that the labor of a human being

---

[1] American Federationist, November, 1914, p. 971.

is not a commodity, "is the Industrial Magna
Charta upon which the working people will
rear their structure of industrial freedom."[1]
The "New York World" beheld the event as
"the most impressive legislative reversal of
judicial decisions that has taken place in this
country since the Dred Scott Judgment was
overturned by the Civil War." The "Federationist" was complacent:

**GREAT
EXPECTATIONS**

> "This law precludes the possibility of
> any similar suit being brought in the fed-
> eral courts for the exercise of normal
> activities as performed by the Hatters—
> and thus the American Federation of La-
> bor has performed its full duties to the
> Hatters and to all labor in the premises."

Mr. Tumulty wrote Mr. Gompers on October 15th, 1914:

> "I take pleasure in sending you here-
> with one of the pens used by the Presi-
> dent in signing" this bill. The pen was
> "added to the collection of famous pens
> at the A. F. of L. Headquarters" and
> "will be given the place of greatest
> honor", because "it is symbolic of the
> most comprehensive and most fundamen-
> tal legislation in behalf of human liberty
> that has been enacted anywhere in the
> world."[2]

During this same period, when politicians

---

[1] American Federationist, November, 1914, pp. 971-2.
[2]   "   "   "   1914, pp. 973-4.

were so suppliant and pliant in their relations to labor unions, a few other laws of similar nature were passed in some of the states, but so far as they played any conspicuous part in the history of this subject, we need refer only specifically to the Massachusetts Anti-Injunction law enacted in July, 1914, the Arizona Anti-Injunction law, enacted in 1913. Each of these, as well as the Clayton Act, commands attention, not for itself alone, but for the mishaps which befell it.

THE RIGHT TO LABOR

To understand the fate of these measures, we must bear in mind the simple and fundamental concept against which organized labor was directing its energies. In the latter part of the 18th century Turgot declared:

> "God made the right to labor the property of every man since he gave to him needs and referred him to labor as the necessary means for satisfying these needs, and this property is the first, the holiest, the most imprescriptible."

A century or more later, the Supreme Court of the United States and State Supreme Courts were repeatedly declaring what from sheer common sense and the immutable nature of inherent facts they could not avoid holding,—that the right to earn a livelihood, whether it be the right of the workman to pursue his trade or the right of an employer to operate his business, is as much a property right as the tangible dollars with which one thereby fills his purse. Jurists agree on this fundamental, and grant these rights the same measure of protection they vouchsafe to other property rights, remarking it would be far less serious to deny protection to the goodwill or tangible property of business than to the workman's right to work.

The legal protection of these inalienable rights being the fortress to which non-unionists flee for protection, the artillery of the unions has been directed to the demolition of this fortress, because it lies athwart their path to more complete conquest. The end sought was the right to enlarge the union army by conscription. The scheme was to confiscate whatever property interest the workman or employer has in this industrial franchise. The method of confiscation was to be a process of political legerdemain whereby through legislation this right to work should be transmuted from a property right into something which is not a property right. Bills were, therefore, systematically introduced and pushed in Congress and state legislatures declaring that the right to enter into the relation of employer and employe or to carry on business, or to labor, shall not be construed as a property right. Thus we come to the popular

CONFISCATE THE RIGHT TO LABOR

declaration that "the labor of a human being is not a commodity or article of commerce."

Curiously enough that conservative old champion of individual rights, the Commonwealth of Massachusetts, was almost the first State to respond to this campaign by enacting such a law. July 4th would have been the appropriate day for it to lay the axe at the root of the tree of liberty, but the law did not pass until July 7th, 1914.

THE I. W. W. SEEKS AN INJUNCTION

Shortly, thereafter, a branch of the Industrial Workers of the World sought an injunction against the Hod Carriers' Union of the American Federation of Labor because that union had conspired to drive the members of the I. W. W. from their jobs by calling strikes of various trades upon buildings where they were employed. Under such a regime the Hod Carriers' Union, being affiliated with the unions of other trades, were in absolute control, unless the law intervened. If the right to work were no longer a property right, as declared by the newly enacted law of that State, the complainants were helpless, but if the right to work were to be regarded as it had been regarded in the past, an injunction should issue. In 1916 the case was decided by the highest court of Massachusetts. It held the law to be unconstitutional, saying:

"The right to make contracts to earn

money by labor is at least as essential to the laborer as is any property right to other members of society. If as much protection is not given by the laws to this property, which often may be the owner's only substantial asset, as is given other kinds of property, the laborer stands on a plane inferior to that of other property owners."[1]

If a laborer must stand helpless in a court while others there receive protection for their property rights, then the constitutional guaranty of equal protection of the laws is violated.

This decision created an uproar in the ranks of labor. The "Federationist" for August, 1916, in an article entitled "Americans, Wake Up!" speaks of it as the baldest usurpation. Another whole article is devoted to the subject under the caption "What Shall be Done with Judges who Violate the Constitutional Rights of Labor?" And Mr. Gompers in an editorial, after his own inimitable style declares, that the "Massachusetts Court filches labor's rights." "Filches them," the court might reply, "of their right to filch the rights of brother laborers."

THE COURTS ATTACKED

Punishment was promised the courts:

"The organized labor movement will see to it that the judges either learn their lesson or that they are removed from

---

[1] Bogni v. Perotti, Mass., 112 N. E. 853.

places so potential for injustice; that the people through their legislatures will restore to the workers—the masses of the people—the rights and the freedom of which the Massachusetts court has undertaken to rob them."

It is significant indeed that the Massachusetts case, which struck at the heart of the model anti-injunction bill, and evoked this cry of defiance, was not a case brought by capital, but a case brought by members of one union, to protect their right to join a union of their own choosing.

THE COURTS DEFIED

When the delegates of the Federation of Labor met in convention in Baltimore in November of the same year, their minds and their emotions were surcharged with this same subject. A solution presented itself. If mere legislation could not by some precious alchemy change that which was a property right into something which was not a property right, they must try a stronger chemistry and alter the Constitution. The convention went on record in favor of a constitutional amendment declaring "that the labor of a human being is not a commodity or article of commerce; and the legislature shall not pass a law nor the courts construe any law of the state contrary to this declaration."

But the convention did not halt there. It

unanimously declared that all judges who issued injunctions of this kind should be impeached; that their orders should be "wholly and absolutely treated as usurpation and disregarded, let the consequences be what they may." Here is something to give us pause. This was no secret session. This was no action of a few mad anarchists. This was a convention of hundreds of men representing two million of the better class of workers, publicly and deliberately adopting a seditious program of concerted resistance to law. From that date to the present time this policy of official defiance of injunctions has been a part of the official program of the Federation of Labor and when President Wilson addressed the Federation at Buffalo in June, 1917, and expressed his confidence in its patriotism, that same convention reiterated its policy of court defiance. There are strange contradictions in our modern life.

Meanwhile "Labor's Magna Charta"—the Clayton Act—which was to introduce "a new era," was put to the test.

The President of the United States had declared that this did not legalize the secondary boycott. The Committee in Congress had declared the same. But the Federation of Labor announced that it had at last done its duty to organized labor by restoring to organized labor the right to do those things which had been condemned in the Debs case, the Buck's Stove & Range Co. case, and the Hatters' case. That point must be decided by the courts.

DUPLEX PRINTING PRESS CO.

Just prior to the enactment of the Clayton Act, events took place which led to its interpretation. The Duplex Printing Press Co., of Battle Creek, a member of the American Anti-Boycott Association, withstanding all appeals of the Machinists' Union, insisted upon operating an open shop. The union thereupon called a strike and picketed the plant, with the result that about five per cent of the employes quit work while the balance went on producing printing presses. Being thus unsuccessful in its attempt seriously to impair the productive organization of this company, the union undertook to prevent, the sale and distribution of its products and issued orders that these printing presses were to be held up in the labor world as a kind of contraband of commerce. All labor in all parts of the United States was to suspend work wherever these presses appeared. Customers were liable to sympathetic strikes at the hands of workers who were called upon to load, haul, handle, assemble, operate or repair such presses and breakdowns were to be frequent. The National Exposition Company, holding an exhibition of machinery at the Grand Central

Palace in New York City, was threatened with a strike against its two hundred exhibitors if it allowed the Duplex Company to exhibit. As these activities were carried on in part at the instance of unionized manufacturers of presses, it was no longer a case of Labor against Capital, but a case of the open shop organization of the Duplex Printing Press Company, with its ninety-five per cent of employes who refused to go on strike, on the one hand and the union manufacturers with their union employes, on the other hand, each striving to market their product and the union combination resorting to obstructive tactics.

THE DUPLEX CASE

In April, 1914, an injunction secured by the Duplex Co. in the Federal Court to prevent a tie-up of the National exhibition at the Grand Central Palace, was first stamped on and defied by the business agents, but union headquarters gave wiser counsels and the exhibition was permitted to proceed. Other activities of the unions were also involved which suit went through several important stages before it was finally decided by the United States Supreme Court in January, 1921.

THE DECISION

The Supreme Court reviewed the so-called Magna Charta of Labor, as it was embodied in the Clayton Act, and found in effect, that it did not substantially alter the doctrine of the Hatters' case or any other decisions.

"There is nothing here," said the Court, "to justify defendants or the organizations they represent, in using either threats or persuasion to bring about strikes or a cessation of work on the part of employes of complainant's customers, * * * with the object of compelling such customers to withdraw or refrain from commercial relations with complainant. * * * To instigate a sympathetic strike in aid of a secondary boycott cannot be deemed peaceful and lawful persuasion."[1]

In describing the conduct of the union, it said:

"An ordinary controversy in a manufacturing establishment, said to concern the terms or conditions of employment there, has been held a sufficient occasion for imposing a general embargo upon the products of the establishment and a nationwide blockade of the channels of interstate commerce against them, carried out by inciting sympathetic strikes and a secondary boycott against complainant's customers, to the great and incalculable damage of many innocent people far remote from any connection with or control over the original and actual dispute—people constituting, indeed, the general public upon whom the cost must ultimately fall, and whose vital interest in unobstructed commerce constituted the prime and paramount concern of Congress in enacting the anti-trust laws, of which the section

[1] Duplex Ptg. Press Co. v. Deering, 254 U. S. 443.

86

under consideration forms after all a part."[1]

The enabling provisions of the Clayton Act relate only to industrial dispute cases between employers and employes and are not to be extended to sympathetic strikes which injure neutral parties. The privileges enumerated in the Clayton Act are limited "to those who are proximately and substantially concerned as parties to an actual dispute respecting the terms or conditions of their own employment."

THE DISSENT

Well might Mr. Justice Brandeis in his dissenting opinion comment upon the epochmaking character of this decision. "This statute," he says, "was the fruit of unceasing agitation which had extended over more than twenty years. * * * By 1914, the ideas of the advocates of legislation had fairly crystallized."

SIGNIFICANCE

Broadly speaking, the effect of that decision was to declare that the Clayton Act, designed to define employment relations, had not changed the law, as labor had contended, and that the decisions of the Debs case, Hatters case and Buck's case stood unshaken as bulwarks of individual liberty. The broad contention that all labor could organize against all capital was rejected. Class war is not a lawful occupation. Class solidarity is not an economic relationship which justifies con-

---
[1] Duplex Ptg. Press Co. v. Deering, 254 U. S. 443.

certed action by all members of that class to
assist one of their fellows in fighting a member of another class. The privileges of economic action must have a rational connection
with the economic interest of the participants.
A learned jurist has said:

> "A sympathetic strike or a boycott must
> be held unlawful as not within the imme-
> diate field of competition. Persons who
> have nothing to do with the trade dispute
> —non-combatants—cannot be compelled,
> by such means, to take part in the struggle.
> A 'boycott,' as that term is ordinarily
> used, and a sympathetic strike, are at-
> tacks upon society itself. They are only
> justified when revolution is justified."[1]

The Federation of Labor treated the decision in characteristic fashion. "Rights Ju-
dicially Purloined" was the title of its article.
"A blow at the movement for human freedom"
was its substance. But again it was the human freedom of unionists to destroy the freedom of those ninety-five per cent of the
Duplex employes who desired to produce
printing presses.

The editorial speaks of the normal and nat-
ural rights of labor unions, and, in exaspera-
tion at the fiasco of its campaign against
courts and injunctions, declares, "We cannot

---

[1] Kemp v. Division, No. 241, 99 N. E. 389 Ill.

88

admit that the court has a right to define those rights."

Mr. Andrew Furuseth asserted the opinion to be against the "commands of Jesus Christ" because it forbids workers from "bearing each other's burdens."

One would have thought that the opinion in the Duplex case clearly settled the legal status of combinations of that character, but apparently there are those who do not so regard it. In 1921 unionized producers of Indiana limestone were unable to reach an understanding with the Journeymen Stone Cutters as to the terms of a renewal agreement, with the result that the industry established a new set of unions with which it proceeded to do business. The Journeymen Stone Cutter's Union, finding itself unable to resume relations with the producers, finally laid down the rule that none of its members working for builders and contractors in the various cities throughout the United States should be allowed to handle or work upon the stone produced by those whom they termed antagonistic workers. They declared that if their members were not good enough to produce the stone, they were not good enough to finish it at the building where it was being used. The result was that the purchasers of stone suffering loss of business because of strikes called against their

THE STONECUTTER

customers, applied to the federal court for an injunction which was denied. The case is now before the United States Circuit Court of Appeals for the Seventh Circuit. There is no issue of fact, but the unions contend that, as long as they maintain no unfair list and do not enlist the co-operation of other trades, they have the legal and moral right to forbid members from working on this product, even though it amounts to a strike against the complainant's customers. It will be some time before this case is finally settled, but in the meanwhile, it is difficult to see any distinction in principle between it and the Duplex case.

ANTI-INJUNCTION CASE

The Arizona anti-injunction law proved as ineffective as the Massachusetts law and the Clayton Act. A restaurant keeper in Bisbee, sought an injunction against pickets patrolling his establishment. They carried banners and distributed circulars and announced in loud terms that the place was unfair; customers were intercepted and annoyed; the circulars told of "graveyard stews" and announced "all ye who enter here leave all hope behind."

The Supreme Court of Arizona denied relief because of the state anti-injunction law, and an appeal was presented to the United States Court on the theory that the state statute was unconstitutional. In December, 1921, the Supreme Court rendered its decision by a divided court declaring that any law "which operates to make lawful such a wrong as is described in plaintiff's complaint deprives the owner of the business and the premises of his property without due process, and cannot be held valid under the 14th Amendment." Describing the acts in question, the court said:

> "It was not lawful persuasion or inducing. It was not a mere appeal to the sympathetic aid of would-be customers by a simple statement of the fact of the strike and a request to withhold patronage. It was compelling every customer or would-be customer to run the gauntlet of most uncomfortable publicity, aggressive and annoying importunity, libelous attacks and fear of injurious consequences."[1]

The state's duty does not end with the maintenance of peace and good order, said the court, and it may not withdraw protection from a property right merely because the injury is not caused by violence.

"The legislative power of a state can only be exerted in subordination to the fundamental principles of right and justice which the guaranty of due process in the 14th Amendment is intended to preserve. . . . To give operation to a statute whereby serious losses inflicted by such unlawful means are in

[1] Truax v. Corrigan, 257 U. S. 312.

91

effect made remediless, is, we think, to disregard fundamental rights of liberty and property and to deprive the person suffering the loss, of due process of law."

If the law is viewed as an absolute legalization of such acts, the answer is that the very purpose of the Constitution "was to prevent experimentation with fundamental rights of the individual." And if it is viewed purely as an anti-injunction statute, it is unconstitutional because it purports to take the injunctive remedy away from one class of citizens while leaving it available to others.

PROTECTION FOR BUSINESS

A political commandment thus thundered forth from the greatest tribunal in the world to the legislatures of forty-eight states, "Thou shalt not deny protection to business."

This was the final epitaph for the legislative program of two decades. We do not say it has not borne some fruit in some jurisdictions and with respect to matters of procedure, but the underlying objective of stripping the individual of protection in order to force him into involuntary association with others failed of attainment.

The Federation was not pleased. It placed the responsibility with predatory wealth:

"The appetite of predatory powers for the injunctive process and the willingness of a cloistered but not always fearless judiciary to feed this appetite becomes more amazing every day."[1]

The calamity impending from such decisions was described at the Federation Convention with great earnestness:

"The fate of the sovereignty of American people again hangs in the balance. It is inconceivable that such an autocratic, despotic and tyrannical power can long remain in a democracy. One or the other must ultimately give way, and your committee believes that this convention should declare that, as wage-earners, citizens of a free and democratic republic, we shall stand firmly and conscientiously on our rights as free men and treat all injunctive decrees that invade our personal liberties as unwarranted in fact, unjustified in law and illegal as being in violation of our constitutional safeguards, and accept whatever consequences may follows."[1]

The American Anti-Boycott Association did not confine itself to protecting employers. On several occasions it has brought suits for workingmen who were being driven from their trade by the union. The first and most prominent of these cases was brought in behalf of a hatter by the name of Dominick Connors. In 1909, there had been a protracted

DOMINICK CONNORS

[1] American Federationist, January, 1922, p. 47.

strike in the hatting industry, during which Connors, as a member of the union, loyally supported the strike. When the Danbury factories settled, the union assessed thirteen per cent on the wages of those who went back to work for the purpose of supporting striking hatters in other cities. This caused insurgency among a considerable number of the union men. Connors and a few others, who had not received their full share of strike benefits during the strike, refused to pay, claiming the union was indebted to them, and, as a result, was not permitted to work in the union factories where they were employed. As nearly every factory in Danbury was unionized, there was little opportunity for their employment at their trade in that town. On a Saturday night they came secretly to see counsel for the American Anti-Boycott Association, then so-journing in Danbury, for in their eyes, to thus visit the house of the enemy was in itself a doubtful act in such a unionized community. Counsel duly warned them how helpless they were before the union machine and of the ordeal which was before them if they undertook the fight, but they were Irish.

It was useless to start a suit in behalf of all of these men at once, so the case of Dominick Connors was selected and commenced in March, 1910. During the course of this litigation which lasted some four years, Connors had a hard time, and being unable to secure employment in Danbury, finally dug ditches in Yonkers, for wages far under those he had been accustomed to receive. But he never winced or asked for help.

Work was light and idle union hatters crowded the Danbury court room and blocked the entrances when the case came on for trial. Connors had difficulty finding a place to sleep. One boarding house put him out because of union hostility. As he went from the court house with his counsel, he was stoned. The instructions of the court to the jury were so much in favor of the defendants that a verdict in their favor was inevitable, but it was that ill wind which in 1913 brought the case before the Supreme Court of Errors of Connecticut for a decision on fundamentals. It was contended that the combination between the hat manufacturers of Danbury and the unions, providing for the employment of union men exclusively, unduly restricted the opportunities of an individual to pursue his trade, and was against the public good. The Supreme Court of Connecticut upheld this contention:

"Monopolies of things of common use and need, whether created by governmental grant or by the acts of private

THE CONNORS' DECISION

persons or corporations, are odious, and their existence is contrary to public policy. They were condemned by the common law of England, and, although changing in their more common source, have remained under a like condemnation in that country and this to this day. They are especially intolerable where they concern the basic resource of individual existence, to wit, the capacity to labor. The whole theory of a free government is opposed to them. Their beneficiaries may enjoy the favors they bestow, and feel injured when deprived of them. But the interest of the public outweighs that of individuals, and the public at large can see nothing but danger in the monopoly of anything of which there is a common need, or which is a common resource of life. This is an old and familiar doctrine in whose maintenance none have as deep a concern as the poor, the humble, and those who live by the labor of their hands."

This decision became another bulwark of the open shop.

LAW AND LABOR

The work of the American Anti-Boycott Association gradually broadened beyond the conception of its founders. It was dealing comprehensively with the law of industrial relations, and had important activities which were not suggested by its name. In 1919, this new condition received recognition by changing the name of the Association to the "League for Industrial Rights." The publication of a monthly periodical entitled "𝕷𝖆𝖜 𝖆𝖓𝖉 𝕷𝖆𝖇𝖔𝖗" was authorized to review current labor decisions and to discuss matters of special importance in the field of industrial relations, and its columns were finally extended to include an "Industrial Relations Department" which should review important plans or experiments designed to promote better industrial relations. "𝕷𝖆𝖜 𝖆𝖓𝖉 𝕷𝖆𝖇𝖔𝖗" has been continuously published since 1919, and at the end of each year the monthly issues are bound into permanent volumes, carefully indexed, which constitute a valuable record of one phase of our industrial history.

The League was the first national organization to publish and circulate a pamphlet advocating employe representation. With "𝕷𝖆𝖜 𝖆𝖓𝖉 𝕷𝖆𝖇𝖔𝖗" as its mouthpiece, it has earnestly sought to avoid a spirit of class consciousness or prejudice in its utterances and to demonstrate that its attitude was not anti-union in character. **ANTI-UNIONISM CONDEMNED**

In 1920, "𝕷𝖆𝖜 𝖆𝖓𝖉 𝕷𝖆𝖇𝖔𝖗" expressed its opinion of anti-union contracts in no uncertain terms. There was a tendency among employers to adopt contracts forbidding employes to join a labor union or to have any dealings or communications with union men in relation to such membership. Condemning these contracts, an editorial in "𝕷𝖆𝖜 𝖆𝖓𝖉 𝕷𝖆-𝖇𝖔𝖗" said:

"Shall employes be thus driven to sell their birthright for a mess of pottage? Can the resourcefulness of radical leadership devise any means better calculated to influence the workers and the public against the employing class? In the name of justice—in the name of public policy—in the name of many other considerations —let us have an end of this."[1]

The same editorial outlines the League's conception of the principle of industrial liberty in equally unequivocal terms:

"An organization like the League which stands for human liberty and against oppressive restrictions on individual action, believes in the open shop. It defends the right to organize which carries with it the right to remain unorganized and opposes unfair action on the part of employers or labor unions to restrict a worker's liberty in this regard. The closed shop, whether union or non-union, is incompatible with this principle. The employer should not boycott union men and the union should not boycott non-union men. If such principles were adhered to, unions would grow wholesomely in the sunlight of liberty, and the number of their members would depend on service and not on force.

[1] 2 Law and Labor, 166.

If that policy were observed we believe that anti-unionism, which is but the foster-child of closed shop unionism, would never thrive in the United States."[1]

The independent stand of the League upon this question brought a protest from a few employers and led to the resignation of one of its district counsel on June 9, 1920. On the other hand expressions of appreciation of such a fair and independent attitude have been received from time to time. At the outset the League was viewed as a partisan movement, guided by a hostile class spirit, but its performances have done much to overcome that feeling. Of the many testimonials to its fairness of spirit, we quote part of a letter from a member of the faculty of one of our leading universities:

FAIRPLAY

"I have just read 'Law and Labor' for July. Your editorial on Public Policy and Anti-Union Contracts is the fairest exposition of the question which I have read. May I congratulate you upon the strong position that you take and wish you success in securing the adoption of such views by both sides?

"I make frequent use of your valuable magazine in the course in Labor Legislation in this Department of the University and have found it to be not only one of the most accurate but also most progressive in spirit of all the publications

[1] 2 Law and Labor, 166.

representing the employers' associations of the country."[1]

CONSTRUCTIVE LEGISLATION

In 1919 the League extended its program to include the advocacy of new legislation based on fundamental principles which were thought to be in the public interest. That was the first time that a national employers' association had undertaken in a comprehensive way to make constructive suggestions for the guidance of the state and federal legislatures in this field of activity. Hitherto their time had been occupied in an effort to defeat the campaigns of organized labor to wipe out such legal protection as already existed.

The first of these proposed bills was verbatim as follows:

SUABILITY OF UNIONS

"Any voluntary association of seven or more members may sue and be sued in the name of the association."

It had been the law in this country that a voluntary association, whether of employers or employes, or any other group of citizens, could not sue or be sued because it was not an entity. It was beyond the reach of legal process. The League argued that this was not as it should be; that large and powerful organizations exercised a power and influence for good or ill far beyond that which was ex-

---

[1] 2 Law and Labor, 186.

ercised by individuals, and that, therefore, public safety and public welfare required that they should be brought within the reach of the law. Collective responsibility should be an incident of collective action. A number of states in substance, adopted this proposed law, but since the decision of the United States Supreme Court in the Coronado Coal Company case (of which we will speak more at length), holding unions to be suable, the need for it is not as urgent as there is a probability that state courts, not previously committed on this subject, will follow that opinion.

The second bill was entitled, "For the better protection of public welfare against unwarranted strikes and lockouts." It aimed at the codification of the fundamental principles of law and morality underlying militant activities of employers and employes, and applied with equal force to the lockout and the strike. Its provisions, which were limited to about 300 words, comprehensively covered seven underlying principles as follows:

A NEW CODE

The organization of strikes by government employes was declared to be unlawful on the ground that the conditions of employment of such employes presented political questions to be settled by the ballot box. The philosophy of the strike that a single employe is comparatively helpless as against a powerful employer and that, therefore, he must be permitted to organize in order to maintain a balance of power has no application to a governmental employe. No man is supposed to exercise any balance of power as against his government.

The organization of strikes or lockouts in violation of agreement was declared to be unlawful. Labor agreements must not become mere scraps of paper. The statute in this respect bespoke the law as it existed and the ordinary conscience of mankind. In the same manner the bill dealt with strikes in violation of arbitration awards, for these involve a violation of the arbitration agreement upon which the award is based.

Strikes or lockouts to enforce terms of employment were declared unlawful except where the demands involved had been first presented and reasonable time given for their consideration. At the best, industrial warfare should be a weapon of last resort. To enter upon it without warning is like waging war without exhausting the resources of diplomacy. Where the factory organization provides reasonable methods for adjustment and conciliation and the machinery of adjustment is not unduly delayed, no breach of relations to enforce demands should be lawful until these internal methods have been exhausted.

Sympathetic strikes and lockouts were declared unlawful by the phrase that it was unlawful to engage in industrial warfare "where there is no trade dispute involving issues of direct benefit to the acting party." Speaking in terms of law and order and not in terms of revolution, to justify economic militancy, there must be a direct economic relationship and interest, otherwise it is merely class warfare.

The open shop was covered by a clause which made it unlawful to organize strikes and lockouts to prevent or terminate the employment of any person because of membership or non-membership in any labor union.

Strikes and lockouts on public utilities were restricted by a declaration that they were unlawful where the party against whom demands are pending is willing to submit those demands to arbitration. Where the tribunal of reason is available, there is no justification for resort to the tribunal of force.

It is interesting to note how these fundamental principles, applying as far as possible with equal justice to employers and employes, conform to popular thought and popular morality in both national and international affairs. Agreements, like treaties, should be observed. Patient negotiation and frank diplomacy should precede warfare. Arbitration should take the place of combat. Self-determination or the liberty of the individual or the nation, should be protected. Governmental matters should be settled at the polls and not by economic or military force.

EDUCATIONAL RESULTS

These measures were advanced not with the idea that there was any probability of immediate enactment, but with a view to stimulating public discussion and public education on these fundamental principles. In debates before the legislative committees the representatives of unions found it difficult to answer the contention that their organizations should be responsible before the law. Likewise, to oppose laws which restrict strikes in violation of agreement or which declared that negotiations should be exhausted before the Rubicon is crossed, placed the opponent in an unenviable position. The principles of abstract justice underlying these two measures were in most, if not all particulars, of such an unassailable character that it was difficult effectively to argue against them. This bill has been introduced from time to time in the legislatures of eight or ten states, but has never been enacted.

On the whole, the results were all that the advocates of this measure expected. After witnessing the fruitless efforts of the American Federation of Labor to secure the enactment of laws especially favorable to their interests, the officers of the League were too wise to expect favorable legislative action in the near future. The immediate fruits were to be education, and these fruits were generously realized.

The famous Debs case, decided in 1894, although enunciating a doctrine difficult to challenge, was never accepted by the unions. The "American Federationist" declared it was "the worst ever made by such a court so far as the interests of labor are concerned," but held out hope "that labor will find redress in some form or another, and that ere long." Another similar case in the Federal courts contemporaneous with the Debs case, and decided by Judge Taft, was called "a humiliating precedent." The Debs decision upheld the statutory duty of railroads to serve all parties without discrimination, including the duty to haul Pullman cars even though built under so-called "scab conditions," and condemned combinations of workers, by strikes, to compel the railroads to disregard this statutory duty.

THE LONGSHOREMEN CASES

It was not until two decades later that the decision was seriously challenged in practice. not to handle open-shop goods. In the summer of 1920, commerce in New York City was throttled by the Transportation Trades Council, comprising longshoremen and teamsters, which declared:

> "None of the members would handle any non-union goods or any goods transported in any way by firms, corporations, or individuals, who refused to employ union labor or refuse to enter into a contract to transport their goods under union terms."

Union fish were separated from non-union fish, and the latter were left on the docks to rot. The ocean-going steamship companies, threatened by strikes of their clerks, checkers, and others employed at their steamship piers, refused to receive goods delivered by non-union teamsters. The Coast Line Steamship Companies, which were undergoing a strike and were employing non-union men on their docks, were tied up because the unionized teamsters of New York City refused to permit the merchants to deliver goods to the docks or to take freight away from the docks. Undistributed freight accumulated in huge piles.

To meet this crisis, which threatened the city with privation and which challenged the fundamental rights of those who had occasion to ship their freight through the largest port in the world, a Citizens' Transportation Committee was organized, composed of representatives of a number of the leading business and civic organizations such as the chambers of commerce, boards of trade and the Merchants' Association. A Citizens' Trucking Company, incorporated to do the work which the union teamsters refused to do, manned its trucks with uniformed soldiers and furnished prompt and efficient service with comparatively little disturbance. That met part of the problem. It did not make it possible for non-union teamsters to haul freight to and from the unionized overseas lines, because the carriers, under threats of strike, refused to accept or deliver freight involving non-union teamsters. That problem had to be solved by litigation which invoked the principles of the Debs case. Burgess Brothers Company, lumber dealer in Brooklyn, and a member of the League, sought an injunction, in the Supreme Court of New York, against the Trades Council, its affiliated unions, and the overseas steamship companies, claiming all were engaged in a conspiracy to deprive it of its right to fair and impartial service under the Federal Shipping Act. The judge described the situation in unequivocal terms:

> "This seems to me to be a combination **THE DECISION** to gain control over transportation and to blockade the channels of trade against all but union merchandise and against all concerns who do not make union con-

tracts. Such a combination to exclude open-shop merchandise from the channels of trade and commerce, and from the markets of the nation is a conspiracy against public welfare and deprives the public of their sovereign right of choice to purchase such goods as they want, because by artificial methods it keeps such goods out of the market."[1]

He declared as well, that the combination violated the federal conspiracy laws and the Shipping Act, and that the steamship companies, in refusing impartial service, were equally liable.

FEDERAL CASE

The Citizens' Committee also found it necessary to start a similar suit in the federal court. A restraining order issued of like nature but was subsequently vacated. On appeal the United States Circuit Court of Appeals held that the unions and the steamship companies were engaged in a conspiracy in violation of the Sherman Anti-Trust Law, and that the plaintiff was entitled to an injunction. These cases reaffirm the rights of all citizens to receive equal and impartial service from the railroads and public utilities. A contrary decision would have worked havoc with our industrial institutions. It would have accorded to labor unions the absolute right, and in some cases the power, to deprive non-union men of

---

[1] Burgess v. Stewart, 112 Misc. 347.

the service of railroads, street railways, telephones and light. Under the doctrine of these cases, a railroad ticket, not a union card, is still the test of the right to be transported.

The courts have been most emphatic in declaring freedom of contract to be an attribute of property as well as of liberty. A person's right in a contract is as much property as any tangible asset, and is, therefore, to be protected against all who would destroy property. Responsibility for injuring such property extends not only to the man who breaks his contract, but to the stranger or intermeddler who wilfully induces him so to do. That is the legal doctrine which underlies our commercial life and is now being applied to the employment relation. That is a doctrine which the League has been urging successfully in a number of cases.

CONTRACTS

The action for breach of contract is not so important in the world of employment relations, but the right of the contracting parties to be protected against the intrusion of outsiders is fraught with great possibilities. If labor contracts, individual or collective, constitute a limitation on the right of outsiders to instigate industrial warfare, they may be able to write more stability into industrial relations. It is an amazing comment on our industrial life, that in making commercial contracts we class strikes with the acts of God or force *majeure,* as uncontrollable acts for which no one can be responsible and exempt ourselves from liability for delay or non-performance arising from such causes.

CONTRACTS PROTECTED

In the latter part of 1917, the United States Supreme Court was forced to rule on this point. Contracts had been made between a coal operator and his employes, providing that the employe would not join the Mine Workers' Union, and a secret campaign for union membership was carried on by the union among the employes with a view to an organized strike, which ultimately eventuated. The Court held the outside interference to be unlawful and declared the employer "having in the exercise of its undoubted rights established a working agreement between it and its employes, with the free assent of the latter, is entitled to be protected in the enjoyment of the resulting status, as in any other legal right."[1]

From that time on, the views of the various courts throughout the country have crystallized upon this subject and the doctrine has become thoroughly imbedded in our jurisprudence that the organization and support of strikes in violation of contract, whether originating with outside agitators or with employes under contract, is unlawful.

[1] Hitchman Coal & Coke Co. v. Mitchell, 245 U. S. 229.

The importance of this ruling was not missed by the unions. "The decision," said the "Federationist," "is of greater significance to Labor than any other court decision.* * * Can we or any other nation permit the organized labor movement to be crushed out of our industrial life, aye, out of our civic, political and social life?"[1] The decision is "unwise, untimely and trouble-provoking." Then came the call for action: "Get busy. Congress must now undo that decision," or better still, "Capture the Courts."[1]

The anti-union character of the contracts protected by this decision, is unfortunate, but the underlying doctrine seems essential if a basis of co-operation established by mutual consent of employers and employes is to be protected from the destructive influences of the outside mischief maker.

Where the employer has entered into a reasonable agreement with a labor union, or with his employes individually or collectively, organized industrial warfare should not be waged against him for conditions which violate that agreement. It is wrong not only to violate an agreement, but for a third party knowingly to induce a violation of agreement. It is doubly wrong for responsible labor unions

---

[1] American Federationist, March, 1918, p. 225.

PRESIDENT WILSON ON CONTRACTS

to use the power and strength of their organization to make such wrongs effective and profitable. In the Summer of 1920, President Wilson found occasion to express himself on this subject, in his usually effective way:

> "No government, no employer, no person having any reputation to protect, can afford to enter into contractual relations with any organization which systematically or repeatedly violates its contracts. The United Mine Workers of America is the largest single labor organization in the United States, if not in the world, but no organization can long endure that sets up its own strength as being superior to its plighted faith or its duty to society at large."

This legal doctrine for the protection of contracts is also the basis of protection for

ARBITRATION CONTRACTS

arbitration awards rendered on a mutual submission. The observance of the award is part of the contract and sound policy requires that industrial warfare should not be carried on for its overthrow. President Wilson well said:

> "There is one thing we should do if we are true champions of arbitration. We should make all arbitral awards judgments of record by a court of law, in order that their interpretation and enforcement may lie, not with one of the parties to the arbitration, but with an impartial and authoritative tribunal."[1]

[1] Social Control of Industrial Warfare, p. 35.

It was in December, 1921, that the Supreme Court for the first time passed upon the question of picketing. Many state courts had dealt with this subject, about a third condemned picketing in any form, while others sanctioned peaceful picketing.

In 1914, a year of significant events, the American Steel Foundries Company, with mills in Granite City, Ill., filed suit against the Tri-City Central Trades Council for an injunction against picketing in every form. The League had nothing to do with this case but it is interwoven with our story and was built on foundations the League had laid. The District Court held that the pickets in this case, being neither strikers nor representatives of strikers, were but wanton intermeddlers who could not justify their activities as pickets and that, therefore, all picketing should be enjoined. The United States Circuit Court of Appeals held that peaceful picketing was lawful. In the United States Supreme Court the case received special consideration. It was restored to the docket for a second argument, and was not finally decided until December 5th, 1921. A notable fact is that the decision rendered by Chief Justice Taft was concurred in by all the court except Justice Clark. It held that picketing was inherently unlawful, and was properly enjoined.

PICKETING

SUPREME COURT AGAINST PICKETING

"The name 'picket' indicated a militant purpose, inconsistent with peaceable persuasion.*** Our conclusion is that picketing thus instituted is unlawful and cannot be peaceable and may be properly enjoined by the specific term because its meaning is clearly understood in the sphere of the controversy by those who are parties to it."[1]

The decision, however, does not bar the stationing of "missionaries."

"We think that the strikers and their sympathizers engaged in the economic struggle should be limited to one representative for each point of ingress and egress in the plant or place of business and that all others be enjoined from congregating or loitering at the plant or in the neighboring streets by which access is had to the plant, that such representatives should have the right of observation, communication and persuasion but with special admonition that their communication, arguments and appeals shall not be abusive, libelous or threatening, and that they shall not approach individuals together but singly, and shall not in their single efforts at communication or persuasion obstruct an unwilling listener by importunate following or dogging his steps."[1]

The line is as clearly drawn as practicable between the stationing of pickets whose pur-

---

[1] American Steel Foundries v. Tri-City Central Trades Council, 257 U. S. 184.

114

pose is one of interference and our fundamental rights of free speech and free intercourse:

> "We are a social people and the accost-
> ing by one of another in an inoffensive
> way and an offer by one to communicate
> and discuss information with a view to
> influencing the other's action are not re-
> garded as aggression or a violation of
> that other's rights. If, however, the offer
> is declined, as it may rightfully be, then
> persistence, importunity, following and
> dogging become unjustifiable annoyance
> and obstruction which is likely soon to
> savor of intimidation. From all of this
> the person sought to be influenced has a
> right to be free and his employer has a
> right to have him free."[1]

Again liberty wins. The liberty of people
to confer and talk together, the liberty of
people to argue when argument is by mutual
consent, and the protection of liberty against
dogging and all kinds of obstruction and interference; but more than one picket means intimidation and interference.

Emasculated picketing does not please the
Federation. It indulged in self-revealing sar-
casm over the single picket:

> "This lone individual might be permit-
> ted under the Supreme Court decision to

[1] American Steel Foundries v. Tri-City Central Trades Council,
257 U. S. 184,

115

proceed with proper Chesterfieldian grace
and courtesy to announce quietly to the
passing multitude the fact that a strike
existed."[1]

The court "laid down such restrictions as to
make impossible anything approaching effective picketing."

**UNION
RESPONSIBILITY**

If industrial rights are to be secure, all persons and private agencies of every character
which play an important part in industry must
be responsible for unlawful interference with
these rights. If the government is responsible
to the people, then the people and all of their
institutions should be responsible to the government. The League believes this responsibility should extend to associations of
employers and employes which pay such an
influential part in our industrial life and, as
already pointed out, has sought to promote its
belief both by advocating appropriate legislation and by test cases in the courts.

If there is one principle which the entire
history of the world has proved to be in-
fallible, it is that power must be accompanied
with responsibility. For that principle mankind discarded the arrogant doctrine of "The
divine right of Kings" for the safeguards of

[1] American Federationist, January, 1922, pp. 44-5.

representative democracy, but unless democracy observes that principle, it, too, will be found wanting, and as capable of tyranny as any despotism.

Where men gather together in well-defined organizations, electing common officials, collecting common funds and providing machinery for common purposes, they exercise a power for good or ill far beyond that of an individual and should be collectively responsible before the law for acts done in furtherance of those collective purposes. If incorporation is regarded as a condition of collective responsibility, that responsibility is merely optional. Associations themselves must be brought within reach of the law.

In Great Britain, labor unions were criminal conspiracies until 1871, when the law was amended to prevent their criminal prosecution. Unions still continued unlawful combinations in restraint of trade until the legislation of 1876, which was followed by the Taff-Vale decision in 1901, holding that labor unions were suable. In 1906, a wave of misguided sympathy led to the enactment of a law which exempted labor unions from suit. Thus the theory of responsibility which seems so fundamental was definitely rejected by Great Britain as to this class of institutions.

IN GREAT BRITAIN

In this country it was generally held, under the principles of the common law, that no voluntary association could sue or be sued and that, therefore, organizations by refraining from incorporation kept themselves beyond the reach of the courts. More recently the tendency has been to whittle down this technicality. Equity first pointed the way, as it always has done in reforming unjust and anachronistic technicalites of law. It held that in suits for injunctions a few officers or members of an association may be sued as representatives of all, and as an incident to the suit a judgment for damages may be obtained and satisfied from the collective funds. In actions at law for damages only, it remained the rule until recently that an association could not be sued in the absence of statute. To fill this gap, statutes were enacted in about fifteen different states.

THE COAL CASES

But the greatest progress in this direction arose in connection with litigation against the United Mine Workers of America. That organization had for years been engaged in a nation-wide scheme to prevent open shop coal operations in order to protect union-mined coal from open shop competition. The conflicts between the union and the open shop operator in some communities almost assumed the proportions of civil war. In 1914, the

Bache-Denman Companies, including the Coronado Coal Company, were attacked and practically wiped out of existence by the union because of their attempt to operate on the open shop basis. During this same period of time, the union was resorting to methods of violence and intimidation in an adjoining county to obstruct the open shop operations of the Pennsylvania Mining Company. The troubles of both of these concerns were brought to the League for Industrial Rights, which took up the case of the Pennsylvania Mining Company, but, for reasons that need not now be explained, was unable to do more in connection with the Coronado case than tender complete co-operation. Counsel advised that the nation-wide operations of the United Mine Workers, of which the Arkansas activities were believed to be a part, violated the Sherman Anti-Trust Law, and that, under the special wording of that act, an association was suable.

In both of these cases large verdicts were secured. The Coronado case went promptly to the Supreme Court where the League for Industrial Rights collaborated by filing a brief *amicus curiae* on the question of the suability of voluntary associations.[1]

---

[1] United Mine Workers of America v. Coronado Coal Co., 259 U. S. 344.

**UNIONS HELD
SUABLE**

In presenting the case of the Coronado Coal Company to the Supreme Court, counsel pointed to the changed economic conditions and the necessity for collective responsibility as an incident of collective action, but rested their contentions primarily on the federal antitrust law which expressly stated that the word "person" as used in the act included "associations." The Supreme Court in the opinion emphasized the changed industrial conditions, the methods by which courts of equity permit suits against representatives of the unions, and the numerous statutes passed by Congress and the different states recognizing the legal existence of labor unions, protecting their union labels and property, and providing for union representation on statutory boards. With these changed conditions before it, the court held:

> "It would be unfortunate if an organization with as great power as this International Union has in the raising of large funds and in directing the conduct of four hundred thousand members in carrying on, in a wide territory, industrial controversies and strikes, out of which so much unlawful injury to private rights is possible, could assemble its assets to be used therein free from liability for injuries by torts committed in course of such strikes. To remand persons injured to a suit against each of the 400,000 members

to recover damages and to levy on his share of the strike fund, would be to leave them remediless.* * *

"In this state of federal legislation, we think that such organizations are suable in the federal courts for their acts, and that funds accumulated to be expended in conducting strikes are subject to execution in suits for torts committed by such unions in strikes."[1]

Unforeseen consequences may flow from this decision that labor unions are suable. Are they not citizens of the state where located, just as corporations are citizens of the states from which they receive their charters? If labor unions are citizens of the state where located, then corporations and citizens of other states may sue them in the federal courts in cases involving more than $3,000, on the ground of diversity of citizenship. If this be true, the doors of the federal courts are open to suits by or against labor unions where diversity of citizenship exists, even though no federal law is involved, and justice can be secured through the federal courts by and from labor unions notwithstanding the fact that local state courts and juries may be dominated by labor unions or employers, as the case may be. In Herrin or certain regions

IN HERRIN

---

[1] United Mine Workers of America v. Coronado Coal Co., 259 U. S. 344.

in West Virginia this might be of great importance.

It was because of the decisions upholding the suability of unions and the jurisdiction of the federal courts that the League has been able to secure some remedy for those injured in the Herrin uprising in 1922, notwithstanding the fact that the sovereign power of the state was unable to convict the murderers in the state courts. The Southern Illinois Coal Co., which was the company involved in the Herrin riots, applied to the League for Industrial Rights for legal relief. The League advised that the uprising, being but an incident of the national coal strike to tie up the production and transportation of coal, constituted a violation of the Sherman Anti-Trust Law, and that the labor unions, which caused the uprising, could be sued in the federal courts for treble damages. Preparations were accordingly made for suit, but the United Mine Workers on learning of this, forestalled further action by buying out the property of the Southern Illinois Coal Co. for a price which was about $500,000 in excess of the reputed value of that property.

Another situation arose in connection with a woman who was assistant manager of a retail store in the Herrin region. Because her husband served on the grand jury which indicted certain people for the Herrin murders, and because of her refusal without authority to sign her employer's name to a protest against the government's injunction against the Shop Craft strike of 1922, the unions placed her on the unfair list, and caused her discharge. In the meanwhile, she moved to Missouri, and, under the advice of the League, brought suit against the unions, declaring there was diversity of citizenship and federal jurisdiction because she was a citizen of Missouri, and the unions were citizens of Illinois. The defendants contended that the unions were not citizens, but the court found they were citizens of Illinois provided all of their members were citizens of that state. This was one step in advance, but the case did not go further because the unions paid the full amount of actual damages suffered by the plaintiff.

Thus in two instances the League was successful in securing some measure of relief growing out of the Herrin uprising because of the principles of law which had been established in previous cases.

The cases of the Coronado Coal Company and the Pennsylvania Mining Company are still in the courts, and up to the present time both plaintiffs have lost on the theory that unlawful interference with the production of coal for interstate commerce, although it stops the flow of that coal into interstate commerce, does not in itself show an intent to restrain interstate commerce. To show such an intent, plaintiffs must submit evidence that the defendants had in mind something more than the usual purposes of a strike. This the plaintiffs are endeavoring to do in both of these cases.

THE BENEFITS OF OTHER DECISIONS

The importance of this body of jurisprudence protecting industrial liberty, to which the League has made such a contribution, is quite apparent. If the principles of self-determination and home rule are to be applied in industry, if employers and employes are to be encouraged to work out relations of mutual satisfaction without coercive interference on the part of strangers, it is essential that combinations which obstruct liberty and often disrupt industrial relations should not be allowed to interfere. It is only because of the decisions secured from the courts that some of the most progressive and promising plans for industrial relations have been established and are being tried in the hope that, in some cases at least, they are better adapted to the public interests than the class-conscious organization of all workers into one group and all employers in another group. The liberty of the employer and the liberty of independent groups of workers to work out their own industrial experiments in these years of flux and transition is a priceless heritage which has justified itself in many promising ways.

A history such as this would defeat its own purpose if it attempted to cover the details of all that has been done by the League. Cases brought in different states throughout the country, district counsels established in leading cities, routine advice to members, educational campaigns, guidance furnished in cases with which there was no direct connection, the citation of the more important cases of the League in hundreds of other cases—all these things, many of which were inconspicuous at the time thereof, have gone to weave the structure of jurisprudence on this subject, and have made a deep impress on the skyline of our industrial horizon.

OTHER CASES

It is a little over two decades since the League was organized, and these have been decades of legal and political contest with no uncertain results. The decisions we have reviewed show how completely the courts have protected industrial liberty from private interference, while, at the same time, largely upholding labor legislation regulating the labor contract where demonstrated abuses occur.

LIBERTY UPHELD

**EDUCATIONAL
WORK**

The struggle over the issues we have been discussing is, of course, not over. New and important issues are being fought out and the gains already made are under the menace of continued challenge and resistance. The work of the League is more important, comprehensive and varied, than ever before. A broad educational campaign is under way to reach educators and student bodies with literature and good speakers. Hon. William L. Huggins, former Chief Justice of the Kansas Court of Industrial Relations, is now in the employ of the League as Special Attorney and is assisting in this work. Invariably the speakers have been met with respect and interest by both teachers and students, and in many instances a new phase has been added to courses on industry and economics in the institution visited. The opinion is unanimous that the League is performing a valuable function in supplying speakers to balance the ready supply of radical speakers which our colleges have been hearing. These and other methods of education are essential to the maintenance of the structure already erected. It may well prove, however, that the battle ground will change at least in emphasis. For the moment, labor unions make prominent two issues: (1) The amendment of state and federal constitutions to curtail judicial power and otherwise accomplish union ends, and (2) efforts to quell the tide of public opinion which inclines more and more toward the assertion of the right of public protection as against privations inflicted by labor unions.

The real cornerstone of the structure of jurisprudence to which the Federation objects, is our independent judiciary, exercising the power of declaring laws unconstitutional. **THE CONSTITUTION ASSAILED** If, through some change in our institutions, judges can be made to respond to the popular will instead of interpreting the constitution as they find it, then our constitution becomes practically a nullity. If the courts are deprived of their power to nullify laws for unconstitutionality, then minority rights and individual rights will be abandoned to the will of the majority or even aggressive minorities. The efforts of the Federation to accomplish this end have been many and varied. It has sought to bring about the popular election of judges, and to intimidate judges by threats of impeachment. It has sought the enactment of a law providing that any judge who declares a law unconstitutional shall be deemed *ipso facto* to have vacated his office. Another plan provided that, if a court held a law unconstitutional, Congress might re-enact that law, in which event it should be final, notwithstanding its unconstitutionality. Other proposed bills required a greater marginal vote of judges to hold a law unconstitutional.

The Federation holds that "the power of our courts to declare legislation unconstitutional and void is a most flagrant usurpation of power and authority by our courts" and that "the continued exercise of this unwarranted power is a blasphemy on the rights and claims of free men of America." If resistance to its program is not effective, and it should be successful in altering our institutions, it cannot be foretold how much of the protection vouchsafed by the decisions we have been discussing would be wiped out.

ASSERTION OF PUBLIC RIGHTS

The relation of public interests to the labor union movement is one of growing acuteness and increasing concern. When, in 1915, there was enacted the Colorado Industrial Commission Act providing for the investigation of disputes before strikes or lockouts should take place, the Federation wrote an editorial entitled "Invasion by Commission," and declaring that the exercise of such power by a political agency "would sap the militant spirit and the resourcefulness and independence that have made the trade union organizations of America the most powerful and most effective organizations that are to be found anywhere."[1]

[1] American Federationist, October, 1915, p. 854.

When the "New York World" endeavored to ascertain from Mr. Gompers what could be done to confine the "future demands of labor within the bounds of reason and justice if there were a nation-wide unionization of basic industries," Mr. Gompers had no adequate answer. He did not think the worker should "submit his case to the general public for decision, when he knows the general public is exceedingly apprehensive of the slightest inconvenience." When the Adamson Act was upheld by the Supreme Court in March, 1917, the Federation objected to the ruling that Congress had the power to require compulsory arbitration of labor disputes on our railroads. It declared that such a ruling opened the way "for establishment of industrial slavery and a fugitive slave law." The present labor provisions of the Transportation Act of 1920 are also criticized, although the findings of the Labor Board are not enforceable and only act as a guide to public opinion. Naturally enough the Kansas Industrial Court Act, which was an extreme form of governmental regulation, came in for vituperative attack.

Union efforts to wipe out the obstacles to class aggression and to override public convictions as to the supremacy of the public interest and the public safety, present tendencies which must be overcome.

129

UNITED STATES AND GREAT BRITAIN

A comparison between Great Britain and the United States upon these fundamental points presents a striking antithesis for which the League is in a large measure responsible and emphasizes the significance of the work accomplished. England has no laws equivalent to our anti-trust law which prohibit combinations in restraint of trade either on the part of labor or capital. In the early part of the twentieth century after a record of labor litigation somewhat similar to that in this country, parliament enacted statutes which largely removed labor unions from the reach of the courts.

Your reputation may be taken by libel, your body maimed by sluggers, your life taken by violence and your business destroyed, and though those acts be done by an irresponsible agitator in behalf of a labor union with a swollen treasury, the union is not civilly responsible. The principle of responsibility which should pervade all human relationships has been expressly withdrawn from the activities of labor unions by placing these bodies beyond the reach of civil process.

Boycotts, primary or secondary, strikes, direct or sympathetic, whether aimed at the exclusion of non-union workers, the disruption of contracts, the control of public utilities, or the injury of the public, have been sanctioned by statute. No individual has any standing before the English courts on account of interference with his liberties through the use of economic power on the part of labor unions. The non-union man and the open shop employer have been abandoned. The public has no rights against the oppressive use of economic power. Labor contracts are not protected against industrial warfare and labor unions cannot be made legally answerable for their misconduct. Parliament being unrestrained by constitutional limitations, has passed laws which in this country would constitute the most invidious kind of class legislation. Here are five fundamental points of differentiation between the industrial relations policy of Great Britain and the United States.

The results of the British policy do not encourage imitation on the part of the United States. In Great Britain low wages and unemployment are chronic conditions. During the period of the war inefficiency because of union opposition to improved machinery and unskilled labor and union restrictions on output, interfered to such an extent that the unions confessed the necessity for a change of attitude on their part, while at the same time reserving the right to restore their old-time practices at the close of the war. The closed shop regime, which was advocated as a means of securing better understanding between employers and employes, has not fulfilled its promise. Class bitternes, radicalism, and a lack of consideration of the interests of society as a whole, have developed more strongly in that unionized country than they have in open shop America. If we have more lawlessness it is because of our polyglot population. During the coal strike, pumpmen in England were ordered to quit work, and it was not even possible for Lloyd George to secure an agreement for the protection of the coal properties pending governmental negotiations. In this country the pumpmen continue at their posts of duty. In Great Britain a strike of the **Triple Alliance**, including miners, transport workers and railway employes, sought a complete paralysis of transportation and commerce, while in this country the miners and railroad employes have hesitated to carry their cooperation to this point. It is difficult to understand what, in the experience of Great Britain, leads anyone to believe that any section of the United States would be better under a compulsory closed shop system. At least that is the viewpoint of the League for Industrial Rights, which has labored for nearly a quarter of a century to make this country, what it is—a land of Industrial **Liberty**.